THE ULTIMATE BLUEBERRY COOKBOOK

VICKIANNE CASWELL

PUBLISHED BY

4Paws
Games and
Publishing

BRUNO, SASKATCHEWAN, CANADA

The Ultimate Blueberry Cookbook

Written by Vickianne Caswell

Cover Art by 4 Paws Games and Publishing

Edited by 4 Paws Games and Publishing

Formatted and Published by 4 Paws Games and Publishing

First publication

Published March 2018

ISBN-13: 978-1988345581

ISBN-10: 1988345588

Published by 4 Paws Games and Publishing

P.O. Box 444

Humboldt, Saskatchewan, Canada S0K 2A0

http://www.4-Paws-Games-and-Publishing.ca

Publishing logo and name copyright © 2016 All Rights Reserved

Find Vickianne, Freckles and Sherlock Online

Website

http://vickianne-caswell.weebly.com/

http://www.freckles-the-bunny-series.ca/

http://www.sherlock-the-remarkable-cat-series.ca/

Facebook

https://www.facebook.com/Vickianne.Caswell.Author

https://www.facebook.com/Freckles.The.Bunny.Series

https://www.facebook.com/SherlockTheRemarkableCatSeries

https://www.facebook.com/The-Adventures-of-Tipsy-Tail-514438432252826

Amazon Authors Central Page

https://www.amazon.com/Vickianne-Caswell/e/B00D1RL73I/

Buy Signed Copies

http://www.4-paws-games-and-publishing.ca/store.html

Other Books by Vickianne Caswell

FRECKLES THE BUNNY SERIES

TRUE TAILS OF FRECKLES AND HER FRIENDS (A FRECKLES THE BUNNY SERIES COMPANION BOOK)

1: FRECKLES IS SCARED OF SCHOOL

2: FRECKLES AND THE LESS FORTUNATE

3: FRECKLES LENDS A PAW

4: FRECKLES AND THE TRUE MEANING OF CHRISTMAS

5: FRECKLES AND THE COST OF POPULARITY

6: THE FRECKLE MONSTER

SHERLOCK THE REMARKABLE CAT SERIES

1: SHERLOCK, THE CAT WHO COULDN'T MEOW

THE ADVENTURES OF TIPSY TAIL

Coming 2018.

THE ULTIMATE COOKBOOKS

THE ULTIMATE CHERRY COOKBOOK

THE ULTIMATE SASKATOON BERRY COOKBOOK

THE ULTIMATE BLUEBERRY COOKBOOK

THE ULTIMATE MAPLE COOKBOOK (coming 2018)

THE ULTIMATE PUMPKIN COOKBOOK (coming 2018)

THE ULTIMATE BACON (coming 2018)

Table of Contents

Blueberries and You

	Amt. Per Serving	% Daily Value*
Calories	57	
Calories from fat	3	
Total Fat	0 g	1%
Saturated Fat	1 g	5%
Trans Fat		
Cholesterol	0 mg	0%
Sodium	1 mg	0%
Total Carbohydrates	14 g	5%
Dietary Fiber	2 g	10%
Sugar	10 g	
Protein	1 g	
Vitamin A 1%	Vitamin C	16%
Calcium 1%	Iron	2%

*Percent Daily Values are based on a 2,000-calorie diet. Your daily values may be higher or lower depending on your calorie needs.[1]

Proven Health Facts

1. **Blueberries Are Low in Calories, But High in Nutrients**

   The blueberry is a very popular berry. It is low in calories, but high in fibre, vitamin C and vitamin K.

2. **Blueberries are the King of Antioxidant Foods**

---

[1] http://foodfacts.mercola.com/blueberries.html

Blueberries have the highest antioxidant capacity of all commonly consumed fruits and vegetables. Flavonoids appear to be the major antioxidant compounds.

3. **Blueberries Reduce DNA Damage, Which May Help Protect Against Ageing and Cancer**

Several studies have shown that blueberries and blueberry juice can protect against DNA damage, a leading driver of ageing and cancer.

4. **Blueberries Protect Cholesterol in The Blood from Becoming Damaged**

The antioxidants in blueberries have been shown to protect LDL lipoproteins (the "bad" cholesterol) from oxidative damage, a crucial step in the pathway towards heart disease.

5. **Blueberries May Lower Blood Pressure**

Regular blueberry intake has been shown to lower blood pressure in numerous studies.

6. **Blueberries May Help Prevent Heart Disease**

There is some evidence that regular blueberry consumption can help prevent heart attacks.

7. **Blueberries Can Help Maintain Brain Function and Improve Memory**

The antioxidants in blueberries seem to have benefits for the brain, helping to improve brain function and delaying age-related decline.

8. **Anthocyanins in Blueberries Can Have Anti-Diabetic Effects**

Several studies have shown that blueberries have anti-diabetic effects, helping to improve insulin sensitivity and lower blood sugar levels.

9. **Substances in Them May Help Fight Urinary Tract Infections**

Like cranberries, blueberries contain substances that can prevent certain bacteria from binding to the wall of the urinary bladder. This may be useful in preventing urinary tract infections.

10. **Blueberries May Help Reduce Muscle Damage After Strenuous Exercise[2]**

---

[2] https://www.healthline.com/nutrition/10-proven-benefits-of-blueberries#section11

Alcohol Drinks

Blueberry Hard Lemonade

Ingredients

2 Tablespoons fresh blueberries

1 Tablespoon fresh lemon juice

2 Fresh mint leaves

Ice cubes

2 Tablespoons Gin

1/2 Cup ginger ale or lemon-lime soda

Lemon wedges, blueberries on a beverage pick, fresh mint, (optional)

Directions

In a highball glass, muddle blueberries, lemon juice and mint.

Fill glass to the rim with ice cubes. Add gin. Top with ginger ale; stir gently.

Garnish as desired.

Blueberry-Hibiscus Sangria

Ingredients

2 Bottle Riesling wine

8 Hibiscus tea bags

2 Cup blueberry juice

1/2 Cup white rum

2 Cup blueberries

2 Cup fresh strawberries, sliced

Directions

Bring 4 cups of water to a boil. Remove from heat and steep tea bags for 5 to 10 minutes. Let cool.

Combine wine, cooled tea, rum, juice, and berries. Stir.

Serve chilled, over ice.

Vodka Cocktails with Blueberry Ice

Distribute blueberries between recesses of 1 to 2 ice cube trays. Cover with water and freeze for 4 hours, or until set.

Rim 12 margarita or martini glasses with water and sugar. Add 1/4 cup vodka to each glass. Top with cranberry juice and soda water. Add blueberry ice cubes. Serve.

Blueberry Vodka Martinis

Ingredients

1 Liter vodka

1 Pint blueberries, rinsed and dried

1 Cup raspberry flavoured liqueur

1 Lime, juiced

1 Twist lime zest, garnish

Directions

To make the blueberry vodka: Pour out approximately 1/3 of the bottle of vodka into a holding container; set aside. Score each blueberry with a small nick and place into vodka bottle. With the vodka previously set aside, fill the vodka bottle until just below the neck. Add just enough raspberry liqueur to top off the bottle. Let sit in a dark place for 2 weeks.

Martinis

In a cocktail shaker filled with ice, combine 2-parts blueberry vodka, 1-part raspberry liqueur, and a dash of lime juice. Shake vigorously and strain into glass. Garnish with a twist of lime zest.

Blueberry Mai Tai

Ingredients

1/4 Can BACARDI® Mixers Margarita Mix (thawed)

1/2 Cup BACARDI® Superior

1/4 Cup orange juice

1/4 Cup blueberries (pureed)

Directions

Thaw BACARDI® Mixers Margarita Mix for 10 to 15 minutes.

Combine BACARDI® Mixers Margarita Mix, BACARDI® Superior, orange juice and blueberries in a large shaker.

Shake for 15 to 20 seconds.

Strain over fresh ice into a double old-fashioned glass.

Garnish with orange slice.

‡ Serves two to three people.

Blueberry-Mint Rum Cocktail

Ingredients

<u>Cocktail</u>

10 Mint leaves and 1 sprig for garnish

10 Blueberries divided

4 Ounces blueberry juice cocktail

1-1/2 Ounces light rum

4 Ounces zero calorie tonic water

Directions

In a cocktail shaker, muddle the mint leaves and 5 blueberries. Add the 4 ounces of blueberry juice cocktail, 1-1/2 ounces light rum and shake vigorously.

Strain contents of cocktail shaker into a 16-ounce glass filled with ice. Drop in the other 5 blueberries and top with 4 ounces zero calorie tonic water.

Garnish with a sprig of mint and serve with a straw.

‡ Makes 1 serving.

Blueberry Piña Colada

Ingredients

1/2 Cup coconut milk

1/2 Cup blueberries, fresh or frozen

1/2 Cup pineapple fresh or frozen (possibly a little more if frozen)

1/2 Cup ice topped up with water; no water and a little more ice if all fresh fruit

2 Teaspoons honey or less to taste

1 Ounce white rum

Directions

Put everything in a blender and blend until smooth.

Vodka Blueberry Liqueur

Ingredients

1 Cup white sugar

2 Cups Vodka

3 Cups fresh blueberries

Directions

In a 2-quart jar dissolve sugar in vodka. Pour in blueberries and cover the jar.

Store in cool, dark place for 2 months (can be refrigerator). Occasionally shake gently. Strain and serve in cordial glasses, or if you prefer, over ice.

‡ Makes 30 servings.

The Blueberry Rum Smash

Ingredients

Fresh (or frozen) blueberries

1 Tablespoon brown sugar

3/4 Ounce fresh-squeezed lemon juice

2 Ounces rum

Ginger ale

Directions

Cover the bottom of an old-fashioned glass or mason jar with blueberries. (If you're using a smaller glass, make a double layer.) Add the brown sugar and lemon juice and muddle (or smoosh with the back of a spoon) until the sugar is melted. The idea is to break the skins of the blueberries, but not to mash them into a pulp. Fill the glass with crushed ice and then add the rum. Top with ginger ale and stir.

‡ Makes 1 cocktail.

Blueberry-Mint Daiquiris

Ingredients

1-1/2 Cups frozen blueberries

2 Tablespoons agave nectar

Juice of 1/2 lime

3 Ounces light rum

2 Ounces prepared Limeade, naturally sweetened

2 Ounces water

6 Mint leaves

1/2 Cup Crushed Ice

Directions

Add all ingredients in a blender and blend until creamy and smooth. Should a thinner consistency be desired, additional water and/or limeade may be added.

‡ Makes 2 daiquiris.

Blueberry-Mint Juleps

Ingredients

2-1/2 Ounces bourbon

1 Ounce mint simple syrup

1 Ounce mint blueberry puree

Crushed ice

Fresh mint leaves

<u>Mint Simple Syrup</u>

1/3 Cup granulated sugar

1/3 Cup water

1 Bunch of mint leaves

<u>Blueberry Mint Puree</u>

2/3 Cup fresh blueberries

2 Tablespoons mint simple syrup

Directions

Combine bourbon, mint simple syrup, and mint blueberry puree together and shake or stir well. Pour over crushed ice and serve with extra mint leaves.

<u>Mint Simple Syrup</u>

Combine sugar, mint, and water together in a small saucepan and heat over high heat until boiling, stirring constantly. Reduce heat to low and cook for another minute or so, then set aside to cool completely. Remove mint before using. You can do this ahead of time and store it in the fridge!

<u>Blueberry Mint Puree</u>

In a mini food processor or blender, combine blueberries and mint simple syrup until pureed.

Breads

Lemon-Blueberry Bread

Ingredients

1/3 Cup butter or margarine, melted

1 Cup sugar

3 Tablespoons lemon juice

2 Eggs

1-1/2 Cups all-purpose flour

1 Teaspoon baking powder

1/2 Teaspoon salt

1/2 Cup milk

2 Tablespoons grated lemon peel

1/2 Cup chopped nuts

1 Cup fresh or frozen blueberries

Glaze

2 Tablespoons lemon juice

1/4 Cup sugar

Directions

In a mixing bowl, beat butter, sugar, juice, and eggs. Combine flour, baking powder and salt; stir into egg mixture alternately with milk. Fold in peel, nuts, and blueberries. Pour into a greased 8x4 inch. loaf pan. Bake at 350°F for 60-70 minutes or until bread tests done. Cool in pan for 10 minutes.

Meanwhile, combine glaze ingredients. Remove bread from pan and drizzle with glaze. Cool on a wire rack.

Blueberry Bagels

Ingredients

3/4 Cup warm water

4 Ounces frozen blueberries, thawed

2 Teaspoons (1 sachet) dried yeast

1/3 Cup caster sugar

2-1/2 Cups plain flour

1 Teaspoon ground cinnamon

1/2 Teaspoon salt

8 Cups water, extra

1 Egg yolk

1 Tablespoon milk

1/4 Cup white sugar

Cream cheese, to serve

Blueberries, to serve

Raspberries, to serve

Directions

Combine water, blueberries, yeast and 2 tablespoons of caster sugar in a jug. Set aside for 5 minutes or until frothy.

Combine the flour, cinnamon and salt in a large bowl and make a well in the centre. Pour the yeast mixture into the well and stir until mixture just comes together. Turn onto a lightly floured surface and knead for 10 minutes or until dough is smooth and elastic. Place in a large bowl and loosely cover with plastic wrap. Set aside in a warm, draught-free place for 30 minutes or until dough rises by half.

Preheat oven to 180°C. Combine extra water and remaining caster sugar in a large saucepan over high heat and bring to the boil. Reduce heat to medium and bring to a simmer.

Brush an oven tray with oil. Divide dough into eight even portions. Roll each portion into a ball. Push a lightly floured finger through the middle of the ball to create a hole. Flatten ball slightly. Place on oiled tray and set aside for 10 minutes to rise slightly.

Add 4 of the bagels to simmering water; cook for 3 minutes. Use a slotted spoon to turn; cook for a further 3 minutes. Use a slotted spoon to remove and return to oiled tray. Repeat with remaining bagels.

Whisk egg yolk and milk together in a bowl. Brush evenly over each bagel; sprinkle with sugar. Bake in preheated oven for 20 minutes or until golden brown and cooked through. Remove from oven and set aside to cool. Serve toasted with cream cheese and berries, if desired.

Blueberry Bread

Ingredients

1-1/2 Cups packed light brown sugar

2/3 Cup vegetable oil

1 Egg

1 Cup sour milk

1 Teaspoon vanilla extract or 1 teaspoon lemon extract

1 Teaspoon salt

1 Teaspoon baking soda

2-1/2 Cups flour

1-1/2 Cups fresh blueberries or 1 1/2 cups frozen blueberries

1/3 Cup chopped nuts

Directions

In a large bowl, mix ingredients in order, mixing each ingredient as you add it.

Pour batter into greased 9x5x3-inch pan with wax paper in the bottom.

Bake at 350°F for 40 to 50 minutes. Turn oven off and let stay in the oven for 10 minutes. Freezes well.

‡ Refrigeration recommended due to the moistness of bread.

Blueberry Scones with Lemon Glaze

Ingredients

<u>Blueberry Scones</u>

2 Cups all-purpose flour

1 Tablespoon baking powder

1/2 Teaspoon salt

2 Tablespoons sugar

5 Tablespoons unsalted butter, cold, cut into chunks

1 Cup fresh blueberries

1 Cup heavy cream, plus more for brushing the scones

<u>Lemon Glaze</u>

1/2 Cup freshly squeezed lemon juice

2 Cups confectioners' sugar, sifted

1 Tablespoon unsalted butter

1 Lemon, zest finely grated

Directions

Preheat the oven to 400°F.

Sift together the dry ingredients; the flour, baking powder, salt, and sugar. Using 2 forks or a pastry blender, cut in the butter to coat the pieces with the flour. The mixture should look like coarse crumbs. Fold the blueberries into the batter. Take care not to mash or bruise the blueberries because their strong colour will bleed into the dough. Make a well in the centre and pour in the heavy cream. Fold everything together just to incorporate; do not overwork the dough.

Press the dough out on a lightly floured surface into a rectangle about 12x3x1-1/4 inches. Cut the rectangle in 1/2 then cut the pieces in 1/2 again, giving you 4 (3-inch) squares. Cut the squares in 1/2 on a diagonal to give you the classic triangle shape. Place the scones on an ungreased cookie sheet and brush the tops with a little heavy cream. Bake for 15 to 20 minutes until brown. Let the scones cool a bit before you apply the glaze.

You can make the lemon glaze in a double boiler, or zap it in the microwave. Mix the lemon juice with the confectioners' until dissolved in a heatproof bowl over a pot of simmering water for the double-boiler method, or in a microwave-safe bowl. Whisk in the butter and lemon zest. Either nuke the glaze for 30 seconds or continue whisking in the double boiler. Whisk the glaze to smooth out any lumps, then drizzle the glaze over the top of the scones. Let it set a minute before serving.

‡ Makes 8 servings.

NY Style Blueberry Bagels

Ingredients

1 Package of active dry yeast

2 Tablespoons sugar

1-1/4 Cups of warm water

3-1/2 Cups of all-purpose flour

1-1/2 Teaspoon salt

1 Cup of blueberries {tossed in 1/4 cup of flour}

Directions

Dissolve the yeast and sugar in 1/2 cup of warm water (let rest 5 minutes). Mix together the salt and the flour - making a well in the centre. Add the yeast and the additional water to the flour and gently fold in the berries. Knead until you have a soft and elastic dough {either by hand or using the dough hook of a stand mixer}. The dough will look quite purple.

Cover the dough and let rise until doubled (about 1 to 1/2 hours). Divide the dough into 8 balls. Press into the centre of each ball forming a hole, and stretch to form the bagel shape. Let rest 30 minutes.

Pre-heat the oven 425°F.

Bring a large pot of water to a boil. Boil the bagels - 1 or 2 at a time for 3 to 4 minutes (they will float to the top when ready). Place on baking sheet and bake 20 minutes.

Lemon-Blueberry Yogurt Loaf

Ingredients

Loaf

1-1/2 Cups all-purpose flour

2 Teaspoons baking powder

1/2 Teaspoon salt

1 Cup Greek yoghurt

1 Cup granulated sugar

3 Large eggs

2 Tablespoons lemon zest

1 Teaspoon vanilla extract

1/2 Cup vegetable oil

1-1/2 Cups blueberries fresh or frozen

1 Tablespoon all-purpose flour

Lemon Syrup

1/3 Cup lemon juice freshly squeezed

1 Tablespoon granulated sugar

Lemon Glaze

1 Cup icing sugar

1/4 Cup lemon juice freshly squeezed

1 Teaspoon vanilla extract

Milk, if needed to thin out the glaze

Directions

Preheat the oven to 350°F. Grease an 8.5x4.5x2.5-inch loaf pan with butter or cooking spray then flour it.

In a large bowl whisk together the 1-1/2 cups of flour, baking powder and salt. Set aside. In another bowl, whisk together the yoghurt, sugar, eggs, lemon zest, vanilla extract, and vegetable oil.

Add the wet ingredients to the dry ingredients and whisk until combined.

In another small bowl mix together, the blueberries with the 1 tablespoon of flour. This will prevent the blueberries from sinking to the bottom of the loaf. Gently fold the blueberries into the batter.

Pour the batter into the prepared loaf pan and bake for 50 minutes or until an inserted toothpick in the centre of the loaf comes out clean. Each oven is different so baking time could vary greatly. Mine took about 1 hour and 10 minutes to be completely done.

While the loaf is baking make the lemon syrup by cooking the lemon juice and 1 tablespoon of sugar in a small saucepan just until the sugar dissolves and the mixture is clear. Set aside.

Make the lemon glaze by whisking the icing sugar, lemon juice and vanilla extract. This glaze needs to be quite runny, so add milk as needed, about a tablespoon at a time until the desired consistency is achieved.

When the cake is done, remove it from the oven and allow it to cook in the loaf pan for about 10 minutes. Remove from loaf pan onto a baking rack, then place the baking rack over a baking sheet. Poke holes in the cake using a skewer or toothpick then pour the lemon syrup all over the cake. Allow it to cool.

Once the cake is cooled, drizzle with the lemon glaze, cut into slices and serve.

Shtritzlach (Blueberry Buns)

Ingredients

2-3/4 Cups all-purpose unbleached flour, divided, plus flour for kneading

1/2 Teaspoon of salt

1 Cup sugar, divided, plus 1 tablespoon sugar

1 Stick unsalted butter at room temperature, divided

1 Tablespoon yeast

2 Large eggs plus 1 egg yolk

2 Heaping tablespoons sour cream

1-1/2 Cups blueberries (about)

2 Tablespoons chopped candied ginger (optional)

Directions

Mix 2-1/2 cups of flour, the salt, and 3/4 cup of sugar in a mixing bowl add half the butter, mix well, and as Sarah's grandmother did, make a well in the centre. Mix the yeast with 1/4 cup of warm water and stir in. Add the 2 whole eggs and the sour cream, mixing well with a spoon. (You can also put everything in a standing mixer.) Then cover with plastic wrap and let sit for about 2 hours until the dough doubles in volume.

Using your fingers, blend the remaining 1/2 cup of flour and 1/4 cup of sugar with the remaining butter and set aside in a bowl.

Preheat the oven to 350°F and cover two baking sheets with parchment paper.

Dust a baking board with flour and roll out the dough to a circle about 1/8-inch thick, adding more flour if the dough sticks. Cut into 12 3-inch rounds and press at least 12 blueberries into each round of dough and sprinkle with a little of the remaining tablespoons of sugar and the candied ginger if using. Then, cradling the filled circle of dough in one hand, use your second hand to carefully pinch it closed into a 3x5-inch oblong shape. Repeat with the remaining dough and blueberries. Put the buns on the baking sheets.

Brush the buns with the remaining egg yolk, pat the streusel – the flour-sugar-butter mixture – on top of the buns, and bake for about 25 minutes or until golden – don't worry if some of the juices boil over. That is part of the buns' charm. Serve warm or at room temperature.

‡ Makes 12 blueberry buns.

Blueberry Loaf

Ingredients

1-1/2 Cups all-purpose flour

3/4 Cup white sugar

2 Teaspoons baking powder

1/8 Teaspoon salt

1/2 Cup milk

1/4 Cup vegetable oil

1 Egg

1/2 Teaspoon vanilla extract

1-1/2 Cups blueberries

Directions

Preheat oven to 350°F (175°C). Grease a loaf pan.

Mix flour, sugar, baking powder, and salt in a large bowl. Stir milk, oil, egg, and vanilla extract into flour mixture until batter is just blended. Gently fold blueberries into batter; pour into prepared loaf pan.

Bake in the preheated oven until a toothpick inserted into the centre comes out clean, 60 to 70 minutes.

Toronto Blueberry Buns

Ingredients

1 Ounce package active dry yeast

1/2 Cup warm water

3 Cups flour (1/2 whole wheat and 1/2 white even)

1/3 Cup sugar

1 Teaspoon salt

3 Tablespoons vegetable shortening

2 Eggs

1/2 Teaspoon vanilla

<u>Filling</u>

2 Cups blueberries (fresh or frozen and thawed)

1/2 Cup sugar

1 Tablespoon cornstarch, dissolved in

1/4 Cup water

1/4 Teaspoon salt

1 Egg, beaten with 1 teaspoon water for an egg wash

Sugar, for sprinkling

Directions

In a small bowl, dissolve the yeast in the warm water. Let stand until mixture starts to bubble, about 5 minutes.

Sift together flour, sugar, and salt. Place in the bowl of an electric mixer. Add shortening, yeast and water, eggs and vanilla and beat until dough is smooth. Let stand while you are preparing the filling.

Mix filling ingredients in a medium saucepan. Bring to a boil, then lower heat and simmer uncovered for 5 minutes, stirring occasionally, until mixture thickens. Remove from heat and let cool.

On a well-floured surface, roll out dough to 1/8-inch thickness. Add flour whenever dough begins to stick. Cut dough into pieces 5 inches square. Place 1 tablespoon filling in centre of the square, then fold dough over on top and pinch to close. Pinch ends closed. Cover buns with a towel and let stand 30 minutes.

Preheat oven to 375°F. Brush buns with egg wash and sprinkle tops with sugar. Bake until browned, about 16 minutes. Serve warm or at room temperature.

Blueberry Sticky Buns

Ingredients

<u>Dough</u>

1 Teaspoon dry active yeast

4 Tablespoons warm water

1/2 Cup milk, room temperature

1 Egg room temperature

2 Tablespoons sugar

2-1/2 Cup all-purpose flour

1/2 Teaspoon salt

1/2 Teaspoon ground nutmeg

1/2 Cup unsalted butter, room temperature

1/2 Cup cream cheese, room temperature

<u>Filling</u>

1/2 Cup unsalted butter, room temperature

1 Cup brown sugar

3 Tablespoons maple syrup

1 Tablespoon cinnamon

2 Cups fresh or frozen blueberries

Directions

<u>Dough</u>

Using a mixer fitted with the paddle attachment, dissolve yeast in water and allow to sit for 5 minutes.

Add milk, egg and sugar and blend. Add flour, salt and nutmeg and mix for 1 minute to combine. Add butter and cream cheese and knead for 5 minutes on medium speed.

Place dough in a lightly oiled bowl, cover and let rest 1 hour in a draught-free place.

Preheat oven to 350°F.

On a lightly floured surface, roll out dough into a rectangle 1/2-inch thick. Spread remaining filling over the dough, sprinkle with blueberries and roll up lengthwise. Slice dough into 12 equal portions and arrange them in a muffin tin.

Allow to rise for 30 minutes. Bake 30 minutes, and turn out onto a plate while still warm.

Filling

Combine butter, sugar, maple syrup and cinnamon. Spoon a tablespoonful of filling into bottom of each dough cup of a greased 12-cup muffin tin.

Overnight Blueberry Buns

Ingredients

2/3 Cup whole milk

6 Tablespoons unsalted butter, cut into pieces, plus more for the bowl and the tin

1 Large egg

2 Cups plus 2 tablespoons all-purpose flour, plus more for dusting the work surface

1-1/2 Teaspoons active dry yeast

1/2 Teaspoon kosher salt

7 Tablespoons granulated sugar

1-1/2 cups frozen wild blueberries

1 Teaspoon cornstarch

Confectioners' sugar, for sprinkling

<u>Special equipment</u>

An instant-read thermometer

Directions

Bring the milk just to a boil over medium heat in a small pot. Remove from the heat and add the butter to melt. Transfer the mixture to a bowl and let cool to between 105 to 110°F. Add the egg and stir to combine.

In the bowl of a stand mixer fitted with the paddle attachment, combine the flour, yeast, salt and 3 tablespoons of the granulated sugar. Add the milk mixture and mix until just combined. Switch to the dough hook and knead the dough on low speed until it is smooth and elastic about 6 minutes. (You could also do all of this by hand.) Form the dough into a ball and transfer it to a buttered bowl. Cover with plastic wrap and set aside to double about 1 hour. Butter a 12-cup non-stick muffin tin (the cups and the top) well.

On a very lightly floured surface, roll the dough out to about a 12x15-inch rectangle. Toss the blueberries with the cornstarch. Sprinkle the dough with the remaining 1/4 cup granulated sugar, then sprinkle with the blueberry mixture. Roll the dough up into a tight coil, then cut into 12 equal pieces. Set a piece of dough cut-side up into each cup in the muffin tin. Cover with plastic wrap and transfer to the fridge overnight.

About 3 hours before you want to eat, take the buns out of the refrigerator. Let stand until doubled in size, 2 to 2-1/2 hours.

Preheat the oven to 350°F.

Bake the buns until golden brown and set, 20 to 24 minutes. Transfer the muffin tin to a rack to cool for about 10 minutes, then use a small offset spatula to loosen and lift the buns out of the tin. Serve warm sprinkled with confectioners' sugar.

‡ Makes 9 to 12 servings.

Blueberry-Brie Cornbread Biscuits with Honey Butter

Ingredients

1-1/2 Cups all-purpose flour

1-1/2 Cups finely ground cornmeal

1-1/2 Tablespoons baking powder

1 Teaspoon baking soda

1/2 Teaspoon salt

1-1/2 Sticks (12 tablespoons) cold unsalted butter cut into small cubes

1-1/3 Cups buttermilk + more for brushing

1 Cup fresh or frozen blueberries

6 Ounces brie rind on + cubed

Honey Butter

1/4 Cup honey

4 Tablespoons salted butter at room temperature

Directions

Line a baking sheet with parchment paper.

In a large bowl, combine the flour, cornmeal, baking powder, baking soda and salt. Whisk until combined. Using a fork, pastry blender or your hands, add butter pieces to the flour and mix until coarse little crumbles remain. Pour in the buttermilk and stir with a spoon until just combined, being careful not to overmix. Use your hands if needed to bring the dough together. Fold in the blueberries and Brie. Use a 1/4 cup measure to drop batter onto a non-stick baking sheet, or press dough on a sheet of parchment paper or cutting board, then use a biscuit cutter to shape the dough into rounds. Try and push any cubes of Brie into the centre of the dough. Brush with buttermilk. Place in the prepared baking sheet and place in the fridge for 20 minutes to chill.

Preheat oven to 425°F.

Bake for 20 to 25 minutes or until light golden brown. Serve warm with honey butter.

<u>Honey Butter</u>

Combine the butter and honey in a small bowl. Brush over the warm biscuits.

Blueberry Cream Cheese Swirly Bread

Ingredients

<u>Dough</u>

1 Cup milk

2/3 Cup sugar

1 1/2 Tablespoons active dry yeast

1/2 Cup butter, softened

2 Large eggs

Zest of 1 Lemon

1/2 Teaspoon salt

4 1/4 Cups all-purpose flour Plus extra for kneading/rolling

<u>Filling</u>

10 Ounces frozen blueberries only

1/4 Cup powdered sugar (for the blueberries)

8 Ounce package of cream cheese, room temperature

3 Tablespoons powdered Sugar mixed into the cream cheese

<u>Glaze</u>

3/4 Cup powdered sugar

3 Tablespoons butter, melted

2 Tablespoons heavy cream

Directions

Dough

In a small bowl warm the milk in the microwave at 30-second intervals until warm to touch. Make sure it is not so hot you can't put your finger in. Add the milk to your (stand mixer) mixing bowl with the yeast and sugar. Cover and leave for about 10 minutes until frothy.

Add the softened butter, eggs, grated lemon zest and salt. Add the flour and beat at low to medium speed until soft dough forms, approximately 3 to 5 minutes. Then increase the speed a little more and knead until the dough is soft and comes away from the sides of the bowl.

Knead for 10 minutes using the dough hook, or by hand if you don't have a stand mixer (again, use more flour if kneading by hand so it is not too sticky wet to handle). If after 10 minutes of kneading, the dough is not coming away from the sides of the bowl, add a tablespoon of flour at a time until it does. When ready, remove the dough hook and shape the dough into a nice ball, then cover with a clean cloth and place somewhere warm to let rise for 1 hour. It should double in size.

Whilst waiting for the dough to rise, make up the cream cheese filling by mixing the cream cheese and sugar until all combined, and adding the sugar to the frozen blueberries and mixing well.

When the dough has doubled in size, punch the air out of the dough and turn it onto a well-floured surface.

Divide into 2 equal pieces and then roll the first piece into a rectangle, about 10 inches by 13 inches. Have the longest side nearest to your body as in the photos below. Be sure to dust with flour when rolling.

Use 2x9-inch baking pans, and grease the pans. Place parchment paper in the pans and cut enough so there is an overhang all around of about 2 to 3 inches.

Use half of the cream cheese and spread all over the rectangle, then distribute half the blueberries as evenly as possible.

Taking the longest side nearest to your body, start to roll the dough, away from you as tight as possible. Then push down to seal the edge at the end.

Use a sharp knife and cut off the ends to make it tidy, then divide the roll in half, then each half divide into 4 pieces, so you end up with 8 rolls.

Repeat steps 6 – 9 for the other half of the dough.

Arrange the buns all around and one in the middle. Place them so the seam is closest to the side of the tin, then cover and let rise again until doubled and they are touching each other, about 40 minutes.

Preheat oven to 350°F (180°C).

Bake for 30 to 40 minutes, then remove from the oven. To test if the rolls are cooked through, Tip them out the pan (use a cloth) and tap the base. Especially in the centre. If it sounds hollow, they're done. If not, return to the oven for another 5 to 10 minutes.

While the rolls are still hot, make the glaze by melting the butter and mixing in the powdered sugar until all dissolved. Then add the fresh cream and mix in well. Lift the overhang of the parchment paper up and carefully pour half of the glaze all over each of the bread pans. You may need to use a brush to help distribute the glaze. Leave in the pans until cool enough to tear the bread apart and eat.

Honey-Blueberry Cheese Danish

Ingredients

1 Pint fresh blueberries

1 Cup sweet cheddar, grated

1 Package crescent rolls

Honey

Directions

Heat the oven to 375°F. Line a baking sheet with parchment paper in case any of the honey leaks out so it doesn't stick. Roll out the crescent rolls and separate each triangle. Sprinkle evenly with cheese, blueberries and then drizzle a little honey over each one. Bake for 10 to 14 minutes or until lightly golden in colour.

Breakfast

Sweet Blueberry Muffins

Ingredients

1/2 Cup butter or 1/2 cup margarine, at room temp

1 Cup granulated sugar

2 Large eggs

1 Teaspoon vanilla

2 Teaspoons baking powder

1/4 Teaspoon salt

2 Cups all-purpose flour

1 Cup milk

2-1/2 Cups fresh blueberries or 2-1/2 cups frozen blueberries

Lemon zest

Directions

Heat oven to 375°F.

Grease 18 regular-size muffin cups (or 12 large size muffins).

In a bowl, mix butter until creamy. Add sugar and beat until pale and fluffy. Add eggs one at a time, beating after each. Beat in vanilla, baking powder and salt. With a spoon, fold in half of flour then half of milk into batter; repeat. Fold in blueberries.

Spoon into muffin cups. Bake 15 to 20 minutes, until golden brown and springy to touch.

‡ Makes 18 muffins.

Blueberry Breakfast Cake

Ingredients

Cake

2 Cups all-purpose flour

1/2 Cup sugar

2 Teaspoons baking powder

1 Egg, lightly beaten

1/2 Cup milk

1/4 Cup butter or margarine, softened but not melted

1 Teaspoon grated lemon peel

2 Cups fresh or frozen blueberries

Topping

1/3 Cup sugar

1/4 Cup all-purpose flour

1/4 Cup finely chopped walnuts

1/2 Teaspoon ground cinnamon

3 Tablespoons cold butter or margarine

Glaze

1/2 Cup powdered sugar

2 Tablespoons of milk

Directions

Preheat the oven to 350°F and spray or grease a 9-inch square baking pan.

In a large bowl, whisk together flour, sugar, and baking powder. Cut butter into small pieces. Add egg, milk, butter, and lemon peel; mix just until dry ingredients are moistened. You may need to finish mixing with your hands to get all the flour incorporated. the batter will be very thick.

Fold in the blueberries. Because the batter is so thick, this may take a few minutes. Spread into a greased 9-in. square baking pan.

For topping, combine sugar, flour, walnuts and cinnamon in a mini food processor or bowl. Add butter and process, or cut in if doing by hand, until mixture is crumbly. Sprinkle over batter. Bake at 350°F for 40 to 45 minutes or until cake tests done.

For drizzle, combine the powdered sugar and milk. If too thick, add a few drops of additional milk at a time until it reaches drizzling consistency. Drizzles over the top of the cake and allow to sit until sugar solidifies.

Blueberry-Oat Crumble Bars

Ingredients

1-1/2 Cup rolled oats

3/4 Cup whole wheat pastry flour

3/4 Cup brown sugar

1/4 Teaspoon salt

1 Teaspoon cinnamon

1 Teaspoon vanilla extract

1/2 Cup butter + 2 tablespoons

1 Cup blueberries

Directions

Preheat oven to 350°F.

In a large bowl, combine flour, sugar, oats, cinnamon, and salt and mix until combined. Melt the 1/2 cup of butter and add it, along with the vanilla, to the oat mixture. Stir until moistened. This may take a minute or two! Fold in the blueberries – it's okay if they pop a little bit.

Butter and flour an 8×8 baking pan. Press batter into the pan. Melt remaining butter and drizzle it over the bars. Bake for 20 minutes, then let cool completely – this can take up to 45 minutes! Cut and serve.

‡ Can be kept in the fridge or at room temperature in a sealed container.

Quick and Easy Blueberry Muffins

Ingredients

1-1/2 Cups all-purpose flour

3/4 Cup granulated sugar, plus 1 tablespoon for muffin tops

1/2 Teaspoon kosher salt

2 Teaspoons baking powder

1/3 Cup canola, vegetable, or grapeseed oil

1 Large egg

1/3 to 1/2 Cup milk

1-1/2 Teaspoons vanilla extract

6 to 8 Ounces fresh or frozen blueberries

Directions

Heat oven to 400°F. For big-topped muffins, line 8 standard-size muffin cups with paper liners. For standard-size muffins line 10 muffin cups. Fill the remaining cups with 1 to 2 tablespoons of water to help the muffins bake evenly.

Whisk the flour, sugar, baking powder, and salt in a large bowl. Add oil to a measuring jug that holds at least 1 cup. Add the egg then fill the jug to the 1-cup line with milk (1/3 to 1/2 cup milk). Add vanilla and whisk to combine. Add milk mixture to the bowl with dry ingredients then use a fork to combine. Do not over mix. Fold in the blueberries.

Divide the batter between muffin cups. Sprinkle a little sugar on top of each muffin.

Bake muffins 15 to 20 minutes or until tops are no longer wet and a toothpick inserted into the middle of a muffin comes out with crumbs, not wet batter. Transfer to a cooling rack.

‡ Makes about 8 muffins.

Blueberry Pancake Casserole

Ingredients

<u>Pancakes</u>

2 Cups all-purpose flour

2 Tablespoons sugar

4 Teaspoons baking powder

1 Teaspoon baking soda

1 Teaspoon salt

2 Cups buttermilk

1/4 Cup unsalted butter, melted and cooled

1 Teaspoon vanilla extract

2 Large eggs

1 Cup blueberries

<u>Assemble</u>

6 Large eggs

1-1/2 Cups whole milk

1 Cup heavy cream

1/2 Cup granulated sugar

1 Tablespoon vanilla extract

Pancakes (above)

1/2 cup blueberries

<u>Topping</u>

1/2 Cup all-purpose flour

1/4 Cup brown sugar

1/2 Teaspoon ground cinnamon

1/4 Teaspoon salt

1/4 Cup butter, cold and cut into cubes

Directions

Pancakes

Combine the flour, sugar, baking powder, baking soda, and salt in a bowl. In a separate bowl combine the buttermilk, butter, vanilla, and eggs. Add to the dry ingredients and stir until almost smooth, it's okay if a few lumps remain. Stir in the blueberries.

Heat some butter in a skillet. Pour 1/4 cup of the batter into the skillet. Cook for 2-3 minutes on each side. Let cool completely. Pancakes can be made up to 3 days ahead, store in the fridge.

Assembly

Grease a 9x13-inch baking dish with cooking spray or butter. Place the pancakes in the baking dish, layering them up against each other almost vertically. It may be helpful to cut the pancakes in half and place cut-side down.

In a large bowl, combine the eggs, milk, cream, sugar, and vanilla. Pour over the pancakes, making sure they all are moistened. Sprinkle the blueberries over the top.

To make the topping, combine the flour, sugar, cinnamon, and salt in a small bowl. Cut the butter into the dry ingredients with a pastry blender or fork until the mixture looks like coarse sand. sprinkle over the pancakes.

Chill in the fridge for at least 2 hours and up to overnight. when ready to bake, take out of the fridge and let it come to room temperature while oven preheats. Preheat oven to 350°F.

Bake until golden and centre is set, about 50-60 minutes. If the topping browns too quickly, cover with aluminium foil. Let cool for 15-30 minutes before serving to let it firm up. Serve with powdered sugar, maple syrup and more blueberries.

Blueberry Baked Oatmeal

Ingredients

2 Eggs

1/2 Cup applesauce (unsweetened)

1/3 Cup brown sugar

1 Tablespoon vanilla extract

2 Teaspoons cinnamon

1/2 Teaspoon salt

2 Teaspoons baking powder

3 Cups old fashioned oats

1 Cup milk, non-fat or almond milk

1 Cup fresh or frozen blueberries

Directions

Preheat oven to 350°F. Spray an 11×7 or a 9×13 pan with non-stick cooking spray.

Whisk eggs, applesauce, brown sugar, and vanilla until smooth. Stir in cinnamon, salt, and baking powder. Stir in oats and milk. Gently fold in blueberries. Spread in prepared pan.

Bake for 28-34 minutes until oatmeal is browned and not jiggly in the centre. Cool slightly before serving. Serve with syrup and/or fruit or vanilla yoghurt.

Store in refrigerator up to 2 days. You can also portion and freeze for quick morning breakfasts!

Gluten-Free Banana-Blueberry Waffles

Ingredients

1 Cup almond flour

1 Cup brown or white rice flour

1/3 Cup tapioca starch

2 Teaspoons baking powder

1/2 Teaspoon fine salt

1 Large very ripe banana

1/2 Cup unsalted butter (1 stick), melted

4 Large eggs

2 Cups buttermilk

2 Teaspoons pure vanilla extract

1-1/2 Cups fresh or frozen blueberries

Cooking spray

Salted butter and maple syrup, for serving

Directions

Heat the oven to 250°F and arrange a rack in the middle. Set a wire rack on a baking sheet and place it in the oven.

In a large bowl, whisk together the almond flour, rice flour, tapioca starch, baking powder, and salt to break up any lumps.

In another bowl, mash the banana, then add the melted butter, eggs, buttermilk, and vanilla. Whisk until combined. Pour the buttermilk mixture into the flour mixture and stir until the ingredients are moistened and just combined. Stir in the blueberries.

Heat the waffle iron to medium according to the manufacturer's instructions. Once heated, spray with cooking spray, fill it with batter, close the lid, and cook until the waffle is golden brown (when the steam starts to diminish from the waffle iron, you can open the top and peek for doneness). Transfer to the wire rack on the baking sheet in the oven.

Repeat with the remaining batter, spraying the iron between each waffle. Serve the waffles right away with plenty of butter and syrup.

Lemon Cream Granola Parfaits

Ingredients

1/2 Cups granulated sugar

1 Tablespoon flour

2 Tablespoons lemon juice

1 Tablespoon lemon zest

1 Whole egg, separated

1/2 Cups boiling water

1 Cup heavy cream

1/4 Cup powdered sugar

Directions

In a double boiler over low heat, dissolve sugar, flour, and lemon juice. Stir in zest. Beat egg yolk and slowly stir into the lemon mixture. Beat egg white until stiff and fold into the lemon mixture. Add boiling water and cook in the double boiler until glossy and thick (about 10-15 minutes). Remove from heat and allow to thoroughly cool. Whip cream and powdered sugar until soft peaks form. Fold into the lemon sauce.

Blueberry Breakfast Cookies

Ingredients

2 Cups old-fashioned rolled oats

1 Cup whole wheat pastry or all-purpose flour

1/3 Cup ground flaxseed

2 Tablespoons light brown sugar

1/2 Teaspoon baking powder

1/2 Teaspoon baking soda

1/2 Teaspoon ground cinnamon

1/4 Teaspoon salt

2 Ripe bananas, mashed

1 Large egg, lightly beaten

2-1/2 Tablespoons coconut oil, melted

2-1/2 Tablespoons unsalted butter, melted

3 Tablespoons buttermilk

2 Teaspoons vanilla extract

1 Cup fresh blueberries

1/2 Cup toasted sliced almonds

3 Ounces dark chocolate, chopped

Directions

Preheat the oven to 350°F.

In a large bowl, whisk together the oats, flour, flaxseed, sugar, baking powder, baking soda, cinnamon, and salt. In a smaller bowl, mix together the mashed bananas, egg, coconut oil, butter, vanilla extract, and buttermilk. Add the wet ingredients to the dry and mix them until just combined. Stir in the blueberries, almonds, and the chocolate until they are evenly dispersed.

Scoop out the dough 2 tablespoons at a time and place it on a non-stick baking sheet, keeping the cookies 2 inches apart from each other. Bake for 12 to 15 minutes, then remove the sheet from the oven and let the cookies cool on the baking sheet.

These cookies are best when eaten the first or second day, but can be stored in a sealed bag or container for up to 5 days. I even like them stored in the fridge and you can freeze the dough ahead of time too. I suggest scooping out the cookies and freezing like that. Bake at the same temperature for a minute or so longer if frozen.

Blueberry-Vanilla Greek Yogurt Granola Bars

Ingredients

2 Cups rolled oats gluten-free if needed

1-1/2 Cup brown Rice Krispies®

1/4 Cup shredded unsweetened coconut

1/4 Cup whole roasted almonds roughly chopped

1 Tablespoon chia seeds

1/4 Teaspoon salt

1/2 Cup peanut butter or almond butter

1/2 Cup honey

1-1/2 Teaspoon vanilla

1 Cup dried blueberries

Greek Yogurt Coating

1 Tablespoon water

1 Teaspoon vanilla extract

1/2 Teaspoon gelatin

1/4 Cup Greek yoghurt

1 Tablespoon honey

Pinch of salt

2 Cups powdered sugar

Directions

Line a 9x13 square Pyrex® pan with wax or parchment paper.

In a large bowl combine the oats, Rice Krispies®, coconut, almonds, chia seeds and salt. Mix together.

In a small microwave-safe bowl combine the almond butter and honey. Microwave for 30 seconds to 1 minute or until the mixture is hot and pourable. Add the vanilla and mix again.

Add the honey mixture to the dry oat mixture and mix until everything is moist and combined. Gently stir in the blueberries. Press the mixture into the prepared pan and then using the back of a measuring cup press the mixture into the pan until it is tightly packed. Cover and place in the freezer for 1 to 2 hours. Cut into 9 to 12 bars and return to the freezer.

Make the Greek yoghurt coating. Combine the water and vanilla in a small bowl. Sprinkle the gelatin over top and whisk with a fork until the gelatin is evenly distributed. Set aside for about 5 minutes or until needed. It will set into a thick paste.

In another small bowl, whisk together the yoghurt, honey, and salt. Microwave on 15-second bursts, stirring in between each burst until the yoghurt is liquidy and very warm to the touch. Don't let it start to boil or the yoghurt will curdle. I microwaved mine for 30 seconds total.

Whisk the gelatin into the warm yoghurt mixture. Whisk until the gelatin is completely dissolved. Scrape the yoghurt mixture into a medium mixing bowl. Pour the powdered sugar on top. Use a mixer or whisk until the yoghurt and powdered sugar combine into a thick, but pourable, coating.

Line a baking sheet with parchment paper. Working with one frozen bar at a time, dip the bottom of the bar into the yoghurt and allow any excess to drip off. Flip the bars over so the yoghurt coated side faces up and place on the prepared baking sheet. They will be very sticky. Repeat with the remaining bars. Let the bars sit, uncovered, without touching, overnight or up to 2 days until the yoghurt is dry to touch.

Once the bars are completely dry, flip them over so the yoghurt coated side is now facing down. Drizzle the remaining coating over the bars and allow the bars to sit overnight or up to 2 days until the yoghurt is dry to touch.

Once the bars are completely dry, store in an airtight container at room temperature.

Blueberry Crepes

Ingredients

Crepes

3/4 to 4/5 Cup of flour

1/2 Cup of water

3/4 Cup of milk

3 Eggs

2 Tablespoons of melted butter

1 Teaspoon of vanilla extract

1 Tablespoon of salt

Blueberry Syrup

1/2 Cup of blueberries

1 Teaspoon of light brown sugar

Topping

Fresh blueberries

Vanilla ice cream (or whipped cream/ yoghurt)

Directions

Into a big bowl, combine all the ingredients for the crepe and beat until you attain a smooth mixture. You can store it for 30 minutes or even overnight if you're planning blueberry crepes for breakfast.

Heat a lightly oiled frying pan or griddle over medium-high flame.

Scoop an approximate 1/4 cup of batter into the pan. You can tilt the pan in circular motion to coat the surface evenly and you can have good round crepe.

Cook the crepe for 2 minutes or until the bottom turns light brown. Using a spatula, flip the crepe onto the other side and cook until it is light brown.

For the blueberry syrup, simmer the ingredients over medium-low heat for 10 minutes and let it cool.

For serving, cover your crepes with the desired amount of syrup. If you want, you can also top it with a scoop of vanilla (whipped cream or yoghurt) and fresh blueberries.

Blueberry-Nutella Parfait

Ingredients

Granola

Vanilla or Greek yoghurt

1 Teaspoon of Nutella®

Blueberries

Strawberries

Chopped almonds

Chopped dark chocolate

Directions

Blend the yoghurt with the Nutella®. Place in a cup, layer by layer. Serve.

Blueberry Buttermilk Pancakes

Ingredients

2 Cups all-purpose flour

3 Tablespoons granulated sugar

1 Teaspoon baking powder

3/4 Teaspoon fine salt

1/2 Teaspoon baking soda

2 Cups buttermilk

2 Large eggs

4 Tablespoons unsalted butter (1/2 stick), melted and slightly cooled

Vegetable oil

2 Cups fresh or frozen blueberries

Butter and maple syrup, for serving

Directions

Heat the oven to 200°F and arrange a rack in the middle. Place a baking sheet on the rack.

Place the flour, sugar, baking powder, salt, and baking soda in a large bowl and whisk until evenly combined.

Place the buttermilk, eggs, and melted butter in a medium bowl and whisk until evenly combined.

Add the buttermilk mixture to the flour mixture and stir with a spoon or rubber spatula until the flour is just incorporated and no streaks remain about 20 strokes. (The batter will be lumpy.) Let rest for 5 minutes.

Heat a large frying pan, seasoned cast iron skillet, or griddle over medium heat for about 4 minutes. Test to see if the pan is hot enough by sprinkling a few drops of water in it: If the water bounces and sputters, the pan is ready to use; if it evaporates instantly, the pan is too hot. When the pan is ready, use a paper towel to coat it with a thin film of vegetable oil.

Ladle the batter into the pan: 1/2 cup for large (6-inch) pancakes or 1/4 cup for smaller (4-inch) pancakes, leaving at least 1 inch in between. Evenly sprinkle each pancake with 1/4 cup (for 6-inch pancakes) or 2 tablespoons (for 4-inch ones) of the blueberries. Cook until little bubbles appear on the pancakes' surface and the bottoms are golden brown, about 3 to 4 minutes. Flip and cook the second side until the bottoms are golden brown, about 2 minutes more. Transfer the pancakes to the baking sheet in the oven to keep warm. Repeat with the remaining batter, oiling the pan as necessary. Serve with butter and maple syrup.

Almond–Whole-Wheat Blueberry Muffins

Ingredients

Streusel Topping

1/3 Cup slivered almonds

1/4 Cup all-purpose flour

1/4 Cup packed dark brown sugar

1/8 Teaspoon fine salt

3 Tablespoons cold unsalted butter, cut into 6 pieces

Muffins

1 Cup all-purpose flour

3/4 Cup whole-wheat flour

2 Teaspoons baking powder

3/4 Teaspoon fine salt

1/2 Cup slivered almonds

1/2 Cup granulated sugar

1/4 Cup packed dark brown sugar

8 Tablespoons unsalted butter (1 stick), melted, plus more for coating the pan if needed

1/2 Cup whole milk, at room temperature

2 Large eggs, at room temperature

1 Teaspoon vanilla extract

2 Cups fresh or frozen blueberries

Directions

Place the almonds in a food processor fitted with a blade attachment and pulse until coarsely chopped, about 15 (1-second) pulses.

Whisk the flour, sugar, and salt in a medium bowl until combined. Add the butter and, using a pastry blender or your fingers, cut it into the flour mixture until it's in pea-size pieces or smaller, about 4 minutes.

Add the chopped almonds to the butter mixture and toss with your fingers to combine. Set the food processor aside (there's no need to clean it). Squeeze clumps of the almond-butter mixture between your fingers to form irregularly shaped pieces about the size of kidney beans. Cover and place in the refrigerator until ready to use.

Muffins

Heat the oven to 375°F and arrange a rack in the middle. Place cupcake liners in a 12-well muffin pan; alternatively, coat the wells with butter. Set the pan aside.

Whisk the flours, baking powder, and salt together in a large bowl to break up any lumps and aerate the mixture; set aside.

Place the almonds and sugars in the food processor and pulse until they resemble the texture of medium-ground cornmeal, about 30 (1-second) pulses. Transfer to a medium bowl. Add the melted butter, milk, eggs, and vanilla and whisk until evenly combined.

Add the butter-sugar mixture and the blueberries to the reserved flour mixture and stir until just evenly mixed about 30 strokes. (A few lumps will remain, but don't overmix—the batter will be thick, but the ingredients should be evenly incorporated.)

Divide the batter among the muffin wells (the wells will be very full). Evenly sprinkle all the reserved streusel topping over the muffins. Bake until a toothpick inserted in the centre comes out clean and the streusel is golden brown, about 22 to 25 minutes. Let the muffins cool in the pan on a wire rack for 5 minutes. Remove from the pan and serve warm or at room temperature.

Buckwheat Pancakes with Fresh Blueberries and Maple Syrup

Ingredients

1-1/4 Cups buckwheat flour

1/2 Cup plain all-purpose flour

1 Teaspoon baking powder

2 Teaspoons caster (superfine) sugar

Pinch of salt

4 Eggs, separated

2 Cups buttermilk

Butter, for greasing the pan

2 Cups blueberries

<u>Serve</u>

Plain yoghurt

2 Mangoes cheeked and scored (diced)

Maple syrup

Directions

Heat the oven to 250°F. Place the buckwheat flour, plain flour, baking powder, sugar and salt in a bowl and stir to combine. Place the egg yolks and buttermilk in another bowl and stir well to combine. Add the buttermilk mixture to the flour and mix lightly until just combined. A few lumps are fine, so do not over mix. Place the egg whites in a clean, dry stainless-steel bowl and whisk until stiff peaks form. Using a large metal spoon, fold the egg whites through the batter in two batches.

Heat a large non-stick frying pan over a medium heat and brush a small portion of butter over the base. For each pancake, ladle 4 tablespoons of batter into the pan and sprinkle with a heaped tablespoon of blueberries. Cook for about 2 minutes, or until bubbles appear on the surface of the pancake. Turn the pancakes over and cook for another minute. Transfer to a plate and keep warm in the oven while you make the remaining pancakes.

Serve the pancakes in stacks of three with the yoghurt, mango, and a jug of maple syrup.

Chocolate Chip Blueberry Quinoa

Ingredients

1/2 Cup dry quinoa, rinsed and patted dry

1/2 Tablespoons coconut oil

3/4 Cup canned lite coconut milk + more for drizzling

2 Teaspoons vanilla extract

1/4 Teaspoon cinnamon

Pinch of salt

1/4 Cup mini chocolate chips

1/2 Cup fresh blueberries

Directions

Heat a small saucepan over medium heat and coconut oil. Once melted, add quinoa, and shake the pan to coat, letting toast for 2 to 3 minutes, stirring occasionally.

Combine coconut milk, cinnamon, and vanilla in the saucepan with quinoa and bring to a boil. Reduce to a simmer, cover, and let cook for 15 minutes until quinoa can be fluffed with a fork.

Divide quinoa into two bowls then sprinkle with chocolate chips. Let sit for 2 to 3 minutes so the chips get melty. Add in a few drizzles of coconut milk, then blueberries.

Brownies, Squares, and More

Blueberry Brownies

Ingredients

5 Ounces bittersweet chocolate, finely chopped

6 Tablespoons unsalted butter

2 Large eggs

1 Cup granulated sugar

1 Teaspoon pure vanilla extract

3/4 Cup plus 2 tablespoons all-purpose flour, divided into 3/4 cup and 2 tablespoon portions

1/2 Teaspoon kosher salt

1-1/2 Cups fresh blueberries, divided into 1 cup and 1/2 cup portions

Directions

Preheat the oven to 400°F. Prepare an 8x8-inch baking pan by lining with parchment paper or foil, leaving an overhang over each end.

In a double boiler (or, a heatproof bowl set over a pot of gently simmering water), combine 5 ounces finely chopped bittersweet chocolate and 6 tablespoons unsalted butter. Melt over medium-low heat, using a heatproof rubber spatula to stir occasionally until the mixture is melted and smooth. Once the chocolate and butter have completely melted, remove from heat, and allow to cool slightly on a wire rack.

In the bowl of a freestanding electric mixer fitted with a paddle attachment, combine 2 large eggs and 1 cup granulated sugar. Beat on medium-high speed until light and fluffy, about 5 minutes. Lower the speed to the mixer's lowest setting and add 1 teaspoon pure vanilla extract. Continue mixing at the lowest speed and slowly add the cooled melted butter and chocolate mixture (from the 2nd step) into the mixture, mixing until just combined and the batter is a uniform chocolate colour.

Once the batter is a uniform chocolate colour, sprinkle 3/4 cup all-purpose flour and 1/2 teaspoon kosher salt over the surface of the batter. Use a rubber spatula to gently fold the flour into the chocolate batter without overmixing. Overmixing will lead to dense, hard brownies and me crying tears of sadness. Simply fold until the ingredients are just combined — at this point, it's okay to have one or two flour streaks left in the mixture.

In a separate medium bowl, toss together 1 cup fresh blueberries with the remaining 2 tablespoons all-purpose flour. Add the blueberry mixture to the brownie batter, using a rubber spatula to fold the fruit evenly into the batter. Again, be careful not to overmix!

Transfer the batter to the prepared baking pan and bake in the preheated oven for 30 to 40 minutes, until the brownies are slightly puffed but still moist in the centre. Transfer the pan to a wire rack and immediately press the remaining 1/2 cup of blueberries on to the top of the brownies. Be careful not to press too hard — a gentle tap will do. Allow the brownies to cool in their pan completely before cutting into squares.

Blueberry Oat Bars

Ingredients

2 Cups quick-cooking oats

1 Cup all-purpose flour

1 Cup brown sugar

1/2 Teaspoon salt

1/2 Teaspoon baking soda

3/4 Cup butter softened

3 Cups fresh blueberries

1/2 Cup sugar

1/3 Cup orange juice

4 Teaspoons Cornstarch

Directions

Filling

In a saucepan, bring blueberries, sugar, and orange juice to boil; reduce heat and simmer until tender, about 10 minutes. Whisk in cornstarch and boil, stirring, until thickened, about 1 minute. Place plastic wrap directly on surface; refrigerate until cooled, about 1 hour or up to 1 day before using.

Base/Topping

In a large bowl, stir together the oats, flour, brown sugar, salt, and baking soda. Cut in the butter to form a crumbly mixture. Reserve 1-1/2 cups of the crumbs, and pat the rest evenly into the bottom of a greased 9x13-inch pan.

Spread the blueberry mixture over the base. Crumble the reserved amount of the base/topping over the blueberry mixture.

Bake at 350°F until lightly golden, about 40 to 45 minutes. Let cool completely on rack.

Blueberry Pie Bars

Ingredients

Crust

Non-stick cooking spray, for pan

1/2 Cup unsalted butter, chilled

3/4 Cup sugar

1-1/2 Cups all-purpose flour

1/2 Teaspoon ground cinnamon

Pinch kosher salt

Filling

1 Egg

1/2 Heaping cup sour cream

1/3 Cup sugar

2 Tablespoons lemon juice

1 Tablespoon all-purpose flour

4 Teaspoons Cornstarch

2 Teaspoons vanilla extract

1/2 Teaspoon ground cinnamon

2 Cups blueberries

Directions

Preheat the oven to 350°F. Spray an 8x8-inch baking pan with cooking spray. Line the pan with parchment paper so that it hangs over on two sides. Spray the parchment.

For the crust: In the bowl of a food processor, combine the butter, sugar, flour, cinnamon, and salt. Process until the mixture starts to come together and clump, 1 minute. Remove 3/4 cup and reserve; press the remaining crust mixture evenly into the prepared baking pan. Set aside.

For the filling: In a medium bowl, whisk together the egg, sour cream, sugar, lemon juice, flour, cornstarch, vanilla extract, and cinnamon until smooth. Mix in 1 cup of the blueberries. Pour the filling mixture over the crust, shaking the pan gently to settle the custard and berries. Pour the remaining 1 cup blueberries over the top, spreading them evenly.

Take the reserved crust and sprinkle it over the top of the berries, squeezing the mixture in your hands to encourage large lumps.

Bake for 1 hour. Let cool. Remove the bars from the pan and cut into 9 pieces. Refrigerate until ready to serve.

‡ Makes 9 bars.

Blueberry Crumb Bars

Ingredients

<u>Crumb</u>

3 Cups all-purpose flour

1 Cup granulated sugar

1 Teaspoon baking powder

1/4 Teaspoon salt

1 Cup cold unsalted butter, cut into small cubes

1 Egg

<u>Blueberry Filling</u>

4 Cups (20 ounces) fresh blueberries

1/2 Cup granulated sugar

4 Teaspoons Cornstarch

Juice of one lemon (about 3 tablespoons)

Directions

Preheat oven to 375°F. Lightly grease a 9×13-inch baking pan.

<u>Crumb</u>

In a medium bowl, whisk together the flour, sugar, baking powder and salt. Use a fork or pastry cutter to blend in the butter, and then the egg (the dough will be crumbly). Press half of dough into the prepared pan.

<u>Filling</u>

In a separate large bowl, whisk together the sugar, cornstarch, and lemon juice. Gently fold in the blueberries to coat evenly with the sugar mixture. Spread the blueberry mixture evenly over the crust, drizzling any excess juice in the bowl over the filling. Crumble the remaining dough evenly over the blueberry layer.

Bake for 45 to 50 minutes, or until the top is light golden brown. Cool completely before cutting into squares.

‡ Leftovers can be stored in an airtight container or wrapped in plastic wrap at room temperature or in the refrigerator for up to 4 days.

‡ Makes 24 bars.

Blueberry Squares

Ingredients

<u>Crust</u>

1 Cup white whole-wheat flour or all-purpose flour

1/3 Cup confectioners' sugar

3 Tablespoons cornstarch

1/4 Teaspoon salt

3 Tablespoons canola oil

2 Tablespoons butter softened

Directions

Preheat oven to 350°F. Line an 8-inch-square baking pan with foil and generously coat it with cooking spray.

<u>Crust</u>

Combine flour, confectioners' sugar, cornstarch and 1/4 teaspoon salt in a medium bowl. Add oil and butter; using your fingertips, blend into the flour mixture until evenly combined. The mixture will be a little crumbly. Firmly press the dough into the prepared pan. Bake until just barely beginning to brown around the edges, 15 to 20 minutes.

<u>Filling</u>

Meanwhile, combine blueberries and water in a medium saucepan. Cook over high heat, stirring frequently until the fruit is very soft and mostly broken down, 4 to 6 minutes. Pour through a fine-mesh sieve into a medium bowl, pressing on the solids to extract all the liquid. Pour the strained juice into a glass measuring cup. You need 1 cup strained juice; remove any extra or add a little water if you are short. Stir in lemon (or lime) juice.

Whisk granulated sugar, cornstarch and 1/8 teaspoon salt in a medium bowl until well combined. Whisk in eggs. Stir in the juice mixture. Pour the filling over the crust.

Bake until just set, 15 to 20 minutes. Let cool to room temperature in the pan on a wire rack, about 1-1/2 hours. Gently lift out of the pan all in one piece using the edges of the foil. Cut into 9 squares. Garnish with fresh blueberries and dust with confectioners' sugar, if desired, just before serving.

Blueberry Shortbread Bars

Ingredients

4 Ounces plain flour

2 Ounces caster sugar plus an extra 2 tablespoons

3-1/2 Ounces cold butter cut into several chunks

5-1/2 Ounces fresh blueberries

Directions

Preheat the oven to 350°F (180°C).

Combine the plain flour and caster sugar in a large bowl. Rub in the butter with your fingertips until the mixture resembles breadcrumbs (or you could use a pastry cutter if you have one).

Press about 2/3 of the shortbread mixture onto a lined baking tray (mine measured around 11x7-inches). Be sure to press it in firmly to help it hold together.

Scatter the blueberries across the shortbread, and sprinkle over the remaining breadcrumb-like shortbread mixture. Top with a couple of tablespoons of sugar, and bake for around 30 minutes, until the shortbread is light golden brown and some of the berries have released their juices.

Allow to cool completely, and then cut into squares with a pizza cutter.

Blueberry-Lemon Bars

Ingredients

<u>Crust</u>

Zest of one lemon

1/4 Cup granulated sugar

6 Tablespoons butter, melted

1-1/2 Cups graham cracker crumbs

<u>Filling</u>

2 Large egg yolks

1 (14-ounce can) Sweetened condensed milk (can use fat-free)

1/2 Cup fresh lemon juice

1 Teaspoon lemon zest

1 Cup fresh blueberries

Directions

Preheat the oven to 350°F. Spray an 8×8-inch baking dish with cooking spray. Set aside.

In a medium bowl, combine the graham cracker crumbs, melted butter, sugar, and lemon zest. Stir until graham cracker crumbs are moist. Press crumbs firmly into prepared pan. Bake the graham cracker crust for 10 minutes. Remove from oven and allow to cool to room temperature.

To make the filling, combine the egg yolks and condensed milk in a medium bowl. Stir in the lemon juice and lemon zest. Stir until mixture is smooth and begins to slightly thicken. Gently fold in the blueberries.

Pour the lemon blueberry filling evenly over the graham cracker crust. Bake for 15 minutes, or until just set.

Cool to room temperature, then chill in the refrigerator for at least one hour before serving. Cut into bars and serve.

‡ Bars will keep in the refrigerator for 3-4 days.

‡ Makes 16 bars.

Blueberry Cheesecake Bars

Ingredients

1/2 Cup butter, melted

2 Cups graham crumbs

2 Package (250 g each) Philadelphia® Brick Cream Cheese, softened

3/4 Cup sugar

2 Large eggs

1 Teaspoon vanilla

1 Jar (250 mL) blueberry jam

1 Cup blueberries

Directions

Preheat oven to 350°F. Pour melted butter into the 13x9-inch baking pan. Sprinkle crumbs over butter; mix well. Press firmly and evenly onto bottom of the pan.

Beat cream cheese until smooth. Add sugar, eggs, and vanilla, beating until well blended; set aside. Stir jam in jar until softened. Spread jam evenly over crust; sprinkle with blueberries. Top with cream cheese mixture.

Bake 30 minutes or until slightly puffed. Cool completely in pan. Cut into 24 bars to serve. Refrigerate leftover bars for up to 3 days.

Blueberry Coconut Bars

Ingredients

<u>Crust</u>

1/2 Cup unsalted butter, cold.

1/3 Cup regular sugar

1-1/4 Cups all-purpose/plain flour

1/4 Teaspoon salt

1 Heaping tablespoon lemon curd or blueberry jam

<u>Cake</u>

1/2 Cup softened butter

1/3 Cup coconut milk

3/4 Cup regular sugar

1 Egg (lightly beaten)

3/4 Cup All-purpose flour (sieved)

1 Teaspoons baking powder

1/4 Teaspoon salt

3 Tablespoons desiccated/shredded coconut

1 Cup frozen blueberries (keep in freezer until last minute)

Directions

Preheat the oven to 350°F (180°C) (gas 4) and line an 8-inch square pan with parchment paper, making the sides bigger so you can use the edges to lift it out later.

<u>Crust</u>

Place all the ingredients for the base except the lemon curd in a mixer and mix until fine breadcrumbs. You can also do this using your fingertips and rub in the mixture until breadcrumbs.

Add the crust mixture to the pan and press down, make it firm and then place in the oven for 20 minutes.

While this cooks, place the lemon curd in a small bowl and microwave for 10 – 15 seconds to loosen it. When the crust is done, remove from the oven and using a brush, evenly spread the lemon curd all over the base. Set aside and make the cake batter.

The filling
In a separate bowl, sift the flour, baking powder and salt.

Cream the butter and sugar until a pale light colour. Slowly add the beaten egg, coconut milk and desiccated coconut. If the mixture starts to split, add a couple of tablespoons of the flour. Combine everything, then using a spoon, lightly fold in the flour mixture.

Transfer the batter to the pan and evenly distribute. Take the blueberries from the freezer and sprinkle all over the surface. They will sink a little during baking, so you don't need to push them into the cake batter.

Place in the oven for between 30 – 35 minutes. Be sure to test after 30 minutes if the batter has cooked through by placing a skewer in the CENTRE of the cake and seeing if it comes out clean. All ovens vary and so cook times are never set in stone.

When done, remove from the oven and leave in the pan until cool to touch, then lift out by holding the sides of the parchment and place on a board ready to slice.

Sprinkle with powdered sugar and serve as they are or with a blob of whipped cream!

Cakes

Blueberry Coconut Bundt Cake

Ingredients

Cake

3 Cups flour

1-1/4 Cup sugar

1/2 Teaspoon salt

1 Teaspoon baking soda

1 Cup oil

3/4 Cup buttermilk

2 Eggs

2 Teaspoon coconut extract

1-1/2 Cups blueberries (about 1 pint)

Glaze

1-1/2 Cups powdered sugar (plus more if needed for thickness)

3 Tablespoons milk

1/2 Teaspoon coconut extract

Toasted coconut, for on top if desired

Directions

Add flour, sugar, salt, and baking soda together in a large mixer bowl. Set aside.

Whisk together oil, buttermilk, eggs, and coconut extract in another large bowl.

Add wet ingredients to dry ingredients and mix until thoroughly combined. The batter will be thick and sticky.

Gently stir in blueberries.

Preheat oven to 350°F and grease a 10-inch Bundt pan.

Pour batter into pan and bake for 50 to 55 minutes.

Remove from oven and allow to cool in pan for about 10 minutes, then remove onto a wire rack to cool completely.

When cake is completely cooled, whisk together glaze ingredients in a small bowl. Use a spoon to drizzle it on top of the cake. Top with toasted coconut, if desired.

Blueberry Swirl Cheesecake

Ingredients

<u>Blueberry Sauce</u>

2 Teaspoons Cornstarch

1 Teaspoon fresh lemon juice

1 Tablespoon warm water

2 Cups fresh or frozen blueberries

2 Tablespoons granulated sugar

<u>Crust</u>

1-1/2 cups graham cracker crumbs (about 10 full sheet graham crackers)

6 Tablespoons unsalted butter, melted

1/3 Cup granulated sugar

<u>Filling</u>

24 Ounces full-fat cream cheese softened to room temperature

1 Cup granulated sugar

1 Cup full-fat sour cream (or yoghurt), at room temperature

2 Teaspoons vanilla extract

3 Large eggs, at room temperature

Directions

Adjust oven rack to the lower third position and preheat the oven to 350°F (177°C). Spray a 9-inch springform pan with non-stick cooking spray. Set aside.

<u>Blueberry Sauce</u>

Whisk the cornstarch, lemon juice, and warm water together in a small bowl until the cornstarch has dissolved. Set aside. Warm the blueberries and sugar together in a small saucepan over medium heat. Stir continuously for 3 minutes until the blueberry juices begin to release. Add the cornstarch mixture and continue to stir for another 2-3 minutes, smashing some blueberries as you go. The mixture will start to thicken. Remove from heat and put the mixture through a fine-mesh strainer into a small bowl (to separate the cooked berries and the juice). Keep separated and set both (the cooked berries and the juice) aside.

Graham Cracker Crust

Mix the graham cracker crumbs, melted butter, and granulated sugar together in a medium bowl until combined. Press into the bottom of the prepared pan and only slightly up the sides. The crust will be thick. Wrap aluminium foil on the bottom and tightly around the outside walls of the springform pan. Bake the crust for 7 minutes. Allow to slightly cool as you prepare the filling.

Filling

Using a handheld or stand mixer fitted with a paddle attachment beat the cream cheese and granulated sugar together on medium speed in a large bowl - about 3 full minutes until the mixture is smooth and creamy. Add the sour cream and vanilla, beat until combined. On low speed, add the eggs one at a time, beating after each addition until just blended. Do not overmix the filling after you have added the eggs.

Pour the filling into the cooled crust. Drop spoonfuls of the smooth blueberry sauce onto the batter. Using a knife, gently swirl. If you have leftover blueberry sauce (you will), mix it with the cooked blueberries you set aside. Save for topping the baked cheesecake.

Place the springform pan into a large roasting pan and place into the oven. Fill with about 1 inch of hot water. The foil wrapped around the pan will prevent water from leaking inside.

Bake for 50-60 minutes or until the centre is almost set. Turn the oven off and open the door slightly. Let the cheesecake sit in the oven for 1 hour. Remove from the oven and allow to cool completely at room temperature. Refrigerate for at least 6 hours or overnight (preferred). Loosen the cheesecake from the rim of the pan and remove the rim. Cut into slices and serve chilled. Top with remaining chunky blueberry sauce, if desired. Cover leftover cheesecake and store in the refrigerator for up to 4 days.

‡ You can easily freeze this cheesecake for up to 2 months. Cover tightly and freeze. Thaw overnight in the refrigerator before serving.

Skillet Peach and Blueberry Cake

Ingredients

Cake Batter

1-1/2 Cups all-purpose flour

1 Teaspoon baking powder

1/2 Teaspoon baking soda

1/4 Teaspoon salt

Pinch nutmeg

1/2 Cup butter; softened

3/4 Cup brown sugar; packed

2 Eggs

1 Teaspoon vanilla

2/3 Cup sour cream

1 Peach peeled, pitted, and cut into large chunks

1/2 Cup fresh blueberries or a bit more, if you like

Top of Cake

2 Peaches unpeeled and cut into thin slices

1/2 Cup fresh blueberries

White or brown sugar, for sprinkling over-top

Directions

Preheat oven to 350°F.

In a medium bowl, whisk together the flour, baking powder, baking soda, salt, and nutmeg. Set aside.

In a large bowl with an electric mixer or in the bowl of a stand mixer fitted with the paddle attachment, beat the butter with the brown sugar until light and creamy, about 2 minutes. Add eggs one at a time, beating well after each addition. Add vanilla and sour cream and mix in. Scrape down the side of bowl as needed. Add flour mixture and mix until smooth and well combined.

Fold chunks of peach and 1/2 cup blueberries into the batter, then spread the batter into a greased skillet (10-inch top diameter works well) or a 9-inch cake or springform pan. Arrange peach slices in a circular pattern on top of the batter, around the outside of the cake. Fill the centre with a mound of blueberries.

Bake in pre-heated 350°F. oven for 45 to 50 minutes, or until deep golden and a tester inserted near the centre comes out clean.

Blueberry Gingerbread Cake with Toffee Sauce

Ingredients

3-1/2 Cups flour

1/2 Teaspoon baking soda

1 Teaspoon baking powder

1/2 Teaspoon ground cloves

1-1/2 Teaspoons ground nutmeg

1 Teaspoon ground allspice

1 Tablespoon ground cinnamon

1-1/2 Tablespoon powdered ginger

2/3 Cup molasses

1 Cup milk

1 Cup salted butter

1-1/2 Cups lightly packed brown sugar

3 Large eggs

1 Teaspoon vanilla extract

2-1/2 Cups fresh or frozen blueberries

Toffee Sauce

1 Cup whipping cream

1/2 Cup butter

1/2 Cup firmly packed brown sugar

2 Tablespoon molasses

4 Tablespoon golden syrup or corn syrup

2 Teaspoons vanilla extract

Directions

Preheat oven to 350°F. Grease a large Bundt pan or tube pan well and dust the inside lightly with cinnamon.

Sift together the flour, spices, baking soda and baking powder. Set aside.

Stir together the molasses and milk until well blended and the molasses is fully mixed into the milk. Set aside.

Cream together the butter and brown sugar until light and fluffy, about 5 minutes, add the eggs, one at a time, beating well after each addition. Beat in the vanilla extract.

Fold in the dry ingredients into the creamed mixture alternately with the molasses & milk mixture. Always begin and end with the dry ingredients. When the last of the dry ingredients are almost fully incorporated into the batter, add the blueberries for the final few folds of the batter.

Speed the batter evenly into the prepared Bundt pan and bake for about 1 hour and 15 minutes or until a wooden toothpick inserted into the centre of the cake comes out clean. I generally start checking about 10 minutes before the baking time is up. Using frozen berries will take the longest baking time.

Toffee Sauce

Bring all the ingredients to a slow rolling boil for about 2 minutes before serving over slices of the cake.

‡ Toffee sauce makes about 2 cups.

Cookies

Blueberry Cookies

Ingredients

2-1/2 Cups all-purpose flour

2 Teaspoons baking powder

1 Pinch salt

1/2 Cup butter

1 Cup white sugar

2 Eggs, beaten

1/2 Teaspoon lemon extract

1/2 Cup milk

1 Cup fresh blueberries

Directions

Preheat oven to 375°F (190°C). Grease cookie sheet.

Sift together flour, baking powder and salt.

In a large bowl, cream butter, or margarine with sugar. Beat in eggs and lemon flavouring. Mix in milk and flour mixture alternately in three parts, starting with the milk. Gently mix in blueberries.

Drop batter by tablespoons onto prepared sheets 1-1/2 inches apart. Bake 12 to 15 minutes.

Blueberry Oat Cookies

Ingredients

1/2 Cup butter, softened

1 Cup packed brown sugar

1 Egg

1 Teaspoon vanilla extract

1-1/2 Cups quick-cooking oats

1 Cup all-purpose flour

1 to 2 Teaspoons ground cinnamon

1/2 Teaspoon salt

1/2 Teaspoon baking soda

1/4 Teaspoon baking powder

1 Cup fresh or frozen blueberries

Directions

In a bowl, cream butter, and brown sugar. Beat in egg and vanilla. Combine oats, flour, cinnamon, salt, baking soda and baking powder; gradually add to the creamed mixture. Stir in the blueberries.

Drop by heaping tablespoonfuls 2 in. apart onto lightly greased baking sheets. Bake at 350°F for 12-14 minutes or until golden brown. Remove to wire racks to cool.

‡ Makes 3 dozen.

Almond Blueberry Cookies

Ingredients

2 Cups all-purpose flour

2 Teaspoons baking powder

1/2 Teaspoon salt

1 Stick (1/2 cup) unsalted butter

1 Cup sugar

1 Large egg

1/4 to 1/3 Cup whole milk

1 Teaspoon almond extract

2 Teaspoons lemon zest, about 1 lemon

1/2 Cup chopped almonds, toasted

1 Cup frozen blueberries, thawed and drained

Directions

Preheat the oven to 375°F.

In a medium bowl, combine flour, baking powder, and salt. In another medium bowl, cream together the butter and sugar using a hand mixer. Add egg and beat to incorporate. Add milk, almond extract, and lemon zest. Stir the dry ingredients into the wet ingredients. Fold in the almonds, then the blueberries. Chill the dough in the refrigerator for 30 minutes. Preheat the oven to 375°F. Using two small spoons, dollop mix onto cookie sheets. Bake until golden brown around the edges, about 15 minutes. Cool the cookies on a wire rack.

‡ Makes about 30 cookies.

Brown Sugar Blueberry Cookies

Ingredients

1 Stick butter, at room temperature

3/4 Cup packed brown sugar

1 Egg

1 Teaspoon vanilla extract

1-3/4 Cups all-purpose flour

1/4 Teaspoon salt

1/2 Teaspoon baking powder

1-1/2 Teaspoons cinnamon

1 Tablespoon milk

3/4 Cup fresh blueberries

<u>Maple Glaze</u>

1 Cup powdered sugar

2 Tablespoons maple syrup

1 Tablespoon half and half

1 Teaspoon vanilla extract

1/2 Teaspoon lemon juice

Directions

Preheat oven to 375°F.

Beat butter and sugar with an electric mixer until smooth. Add egg and vanilla, mixing well until combined, about 2 minutes. Stir in flour, baking powder, salt, and 1-1/2 teaspoons cinnamon with the mixer on low speed. Mix until the dough comes together. Add in milk. If the dough is still crumbly, add milk 1 tablespoon at a time until it comes together. Fold in blueberries gently with a spatula – it is okay if they break a bit. Refrigerate for 30 minutes.

Remove dough from fridge and roll into 1-1/2-inch balls or scoop out with an ice cream scooper. Bake at 375°F for 10 to 12 minutes. Let cool completely.

Maple Glaze

Whisk together the ingredients until smooth. If the mixture is too thin, whisk in more sugar 1/4 cup at a time. If it's too thick, whisk in more syrup or half and half, 1 teaspoon at a time. Drizzle on cookies.

‡ Makes 12 to 15+ cookies.

Blueberry Cream Cookies

Ingredients

1 Cup sugar

1/2 Cup softened butter

1 Egg

1/3 Cup sour cream

1 Small box vanilla pudding mix

1/2 Teaspoon salt

1/2 Teaspoon baking soda

2 Cups flour

1 Cup white chocolate chips

1 Rounded cup fresh blueberries, washed & dried

Directions

Preheat oven to 350°F.

Cream together sugar and butter. Add egg, sour cream, pudding mix, salt, and soda. Stir until smooth.

Add flour 1 cup at a time, mixing until smooth between additions. Stir in white chocolate chips.

Create a shallow well in the centre of the dough, Add in blueberries. Very gently, fold dough over several times, doing your best to not squash the berries.

Drop by rounded tablespoonfuls onto greased cookie sheet.

Bake at 350°F for 10 to 11 minutes. Transfer to a cooling rack.

‡ Makes 3 dozen cookies.

Blueberry Pie Cookies

Ingredients

<u>Cookie</u>

1/2 Cup unsalted butter, softened

1/3 Cup powdered sugar

1 Teaspoon vanilla extract

1/4 Teaspoon salt

1-1/4 Cups all purpose flour

<u>Filling and Topping</u>

1 Cup Wyman's Wild Blueberries, thawed and drained well

2 Tablespoons granulated sugar

1 Tablespoon cornstarch

1 Teaspoon lemon juice

1/4 Cup white chocolate chips

1 Teaspoon vegetable oil

Directions

Preheat oven to 350°F. Spray mini muffin pans with floured non-stick cooking spray.

Place butter in the bowl of a stand mixer fitted with the paddle attachment. (You can also use a hand mixer.) Beat butter until it's smooth, then beat in powdered sugar. Beat in vanilla and salt and then slowly mix in flour. Beat until batter forms.

Drop 1 tablespoon balls of cookie dough into each mini muffin pan cavity. Press it up the sides of the pan, creating a crust.

Drain blueberries well. Toss with sugar, cornstarch, and lemon juice. Evenly divide between the cookies, adding some of the liquid that collects in the bottom of the berry bowl but not too much.

Bake for 12 to 15 minutes, or until the sides start to get golden in colour. Cool completely before removing from pan.

Topping

Stir white chocolate chips and vegetable oil in a small microwave-safe bowl. Heat on 50% power in 30-second increments, until melted and smooth. Add to a small sandwich bag with the tip cut off and drizzle over cookies. Let set before serving.

‡ Can store in an airtight container for up to 3 days.

‡ Makes 18 cookies.

Blueberry White Chocolate Cookies

Ingredients

1 Cup unsalted butter softened

1 Cup granulated sugar

3/4 Cup brown sugar

2 Eggs

2 Teaspoons pure vanilla extract

2 Cups all-purpose flour

1 Cup whole wheat pastry flour

1/2 Teaspoon baking soda

1 Teaspoon salt

2 Cups white chocolate chips

1-1/2 Cups blueberries washed and patted dry

Directions

Preheat oven to 350°F and line baking sheets with parchment paper.

Cream together butter and sugars until light and fluffy. Mix in eggs and vanilla. In a separate bowl, sift together flours, baking soda, and salt. Stir into wet ingredients.

Stir chocolate chips into the dough, then add blueberries, taking care not to mash the berries much.

Scoop dough onto baking sheets. Bake for about 12 minutes, until browned on edges.

Blueberry Sour Cream Drop Cookies

Ingredients

1/2 Cup soft butter

1 Cup sugar

2 Eggs

1/4 Cup sour cream

1/2 Teaspoon almond extract

1 Teaspoon vanilla

1/2 Teaspoon lemon juice (optional)

2 Cups flour

2 Teaspoons baking powder

1/2 Teaspoon salt

1-1/2 Cups fresh blueberries

Powdered sugar for sprinkling over tops

Directions

Preheat oven to 350°F.

In large bowl mix cream together butter, sugar, eggs, and sour cream. Then mix in almond, vanilla, and lemon. Combine flour, baking powder, and salt together in small bowl. Slowly add in flour mixture. Fold in blueberries.

Drop by dough by tablespoon onto ungreased cookies sheet.

Bake for 12 to 15 minutes sprinkle with powder sugar while cooling.

‡ Makes 28 servings.

Candies and Chocolates

Blueberry Gummy Candy

Ingredients

1/3 Cup cold water

1-1/4 Ounce package unflavored gelatin

1 3-Ounce package blue flavoured gelatin

8 Blueberries

1 Tablespoon sweetened condensed milk

Directions

Prepare your candy mould by spraying it lightly with non-stick spray, then wiping it gently with a paper towel to leave just a very thin layer of oil in the moulds.

Pour the water into a small saucepan. Sprinkle the gelatin packets on top, and allow it to sit for 10 minutes to let the water hydrate the gelatin.

Put the pan over medium-low heat to melt the gelatin and stir until it is completely dissolved and smooth.

Pour the melted gelatin into a measuring cup with a spout, and then carefully pour the gelatin halfway into the prepared mould cavities. Gently place a blueberry in the middle of each cavity.

Place the tray in the freezer for about 5 minutes to firm up the gelatin. While that is setting, stir the condensed milk into the remaining gelatin in the mixing cup to turn it an opaque blue colour.

After the first layer has set, pour the opaque gelatin on top of the first layer, and refrigerate the candies to set them completely.

Once set, pull the gummies out of the moulds, and serve. Blueberry Gummies can be kept in an airtight container at room temperature for 3 to 4 days, or for several weeks if you omit the blueberry inside.

Strawberry and Blueberry Butter Candy

Ingredients

1 Cup freeze-dried organic strawberries or freeze-dried organic blueberries

1 Cup pasture butter, room temperature

2 to 3 Tablespoons raw light-coloured honey

Small pinch of unrefined sea salt

Directions

Add freeze-dried strawberries or blueberries to a food processor fitted with the "S" steel blade. Pulse until the strawberries/blueberries are ground into a fine powder.

Over a medium-size mixing bowl, strain strawberry/blueberry powder through a fine-mesh strainer to remove most of the seeds or leftover larger chunks. Set aside.

Fit standing mixer with a whisk or flat blade. Add softened butter, honey, and sea salt to the mixing bowl. Mix on low speed until everything starts to combine. Increase speed to medium-high and whip until creamed and it begins to have a lighter white colour, about 1 minute. Stop mixer and scrape down the sides of the bowl with a spatula.

Add strawberry or blueberry powder to the creamed butter mixture and whip on medium speed until completely incorporated, about 15 to 20 seconds. The longer you mix it, the lighter in colour it will get {light pink or light purple}. If you want bolder colours {dark pink or dark purple}, mix until incorporated.

Prep the pastry bag or zip-top bag. You can use a pastry tip if you have one - Can stick the pastry tip into the corner of a zip-top bag and cut a small hole in the corner of the bag, then pushed the top of the pastry tip through the hole. Otherwise, just cut a small hole in the corner of a zip-top bag.

Using a spatula, transfer butter candy mixture to a pastry bag or disposable zip-top bag. Line a baking sheet with unbleached parchment paper. Gently squeeze the butter candy mixture out of the bag onto the lined baking sheet into little bite-sized dollops. Don't worry about making them look perfect. Immediately place in the freezer until firm, about 1 hour. Carefully remove the butter candies from the baking sheet and store in a mason jar or freezer safe container. Store in the freezer until ready to eat.

Blueberry White Chocolate Ganache Truffles

Ingredients

<u>Chocolate Shells</u>

17-1/2 Ounces dark chocolate

4-1/2 Ounces dark chocolate

<u>Decorating Outer Shells</u>

2 Tablespoons raw cocoa butter

Food colouring, powder

<u>Blueberry Ganache Filling</u>

7 Ounces white chocolate

6-3/4 Ounces heavy cream

1 Ounce freeze dried blueberries

<u>Other Items</u>

Polycarbonate chocolate candy mould

Cheesecloth, to buff mould

Directions

<u>Blueberry Ganache Filling</u>

Process freeze dried blueberries into a fine powder. Warm heavy cream over medium-low heat in small saucepan. Pour warm cream over white chocolate and allow to sit for about 3 to 4 minutes to soften. Gently stir with a rubber spatula until chocolate is completely incorporated. Mix in blueberry powder.

Transfer to a piping bag and chill while tempering the chocolate. This can be prepared quite far in advance but will need to be kneaded in the bag to make it pipable if it cools too much.

Prepare the Molds

If the mould has never been used, you will want to rub a very small amount of the cheesecloth onto the raw cocoa butter before using it to buff the individual compartments.

Once the mould is used properly, you should be able to simply buff. Much like cast iron, the mould will become seasoned with each use. If you must wash the mould (ideally, simply blow it out and buff to keep clean.

Buff each individual mould compartment, getting every corner if your mould shape has them. Buff well. This is time-consuming but critical to a shiny finish and good release of the candy. Once buffed, set aside.

Decorating Outer Shells

If you would like to brush a design on the mould, slightly warm the tablespoons of cocoa butter. I microwave mine for 15 to 30 seconds and stir. Do not overheat.

Add colouring and mix until completely incorporated. Warm as necessary if it solidifies.

Using a clean pastry brush, brush some of the coloured cocoa butter onto the inside of the moulds. It may be easier to allow the butter to slightly cool after warming to apply a better coat. Decorate all the moulds and set aside.

Chocolate Shells

Chop all chocolate into very small pieces.

Before beginning, please take some time to familiarize yourself with the process of tempering chocolate.

Begin by warming the 17-1/2 ounces of chocolate over a double boiler very slowly to 118°F (46-48°C).

Remove from heat and cool chocolate to 80°F (27-28°C) by slowly incorporating the 4-1/2 ounces of additional chocolate, stirring constantly. This may take a while to cool, as chocolate holds its heat for quite a while. Be patient and continue to stir.

Place back above a very low simmer and warm melted chocolate to a final temperature of 88-90°F (31-32°C). Be very careful to not exceed this temperature, as you will have to start the process over if so.

Hold chocolate at this final temperature. I generally remove chocolate from the heat, as it holds for a while. Replace and stir, checking the temperature often as needed.

Filling Shells

Clean a large surface or complete with a baking sheet. Fill the chocolate moulds with the tempered warm chocolate (at its final temperature). Tap moulds to ensure there are no air bubbles. Flip mould over and allow chocolate to exit, leaving a very thin coating inside the moulds. Tap the outside of the mould with a rolling pin or something similar. Get as much chocolate out as possible to ensure a thin, crisp shell.

While inverted, use a pastry or dough scraper to push away the chocolate, leaving you with only the inside of the shells being coated. Flip right side up and make sure excess chocolate is scraped off. It is important to remove all excess chocolate so that the candies all release individually.

Filling Molds

Pipe ganache into the hardened moulds. Fill about 3/4 of the mould. If you add too much, you will not be able to get a good seal and the candy will leak or crack.

Leftover chocolate which can be kept and used for the same process again later. It may 'bloom,' or form a cloudy exterior. This is normal and will disappear when re-tempered.

Capping the Candy

To seal the candies, I find it easier to place the chocolate (still held at its final temperature) into a piping bag. Pipe into each mould and again scrape across the mould to clear excess chocolate. Tap mould to release air bubbles and fill in any gaps with additional chocolate. Scrape again and allow to rest to completely harden. If rushed, can chill the candy for 15 to 20 minutes.

Releasing the Molds

To check and see if the candy is ready, you can look on the underside (which will be the top of the candy when released). You should see that the chocolate had released from the mould. If you see spots that have not, those were likely areas not buffed well or you have issues with your chocolate not being properly tempered.

If you see many or all the shells are not hardened and released, you can try to chill for an additional 15 to 20 minutes.

To release candy, you will flip and bang the mould onto a clean surface very quickly. Don't be too gently and try to hit it without it being at an angle. You want it to slap down with the entire bottom side of the candies hitting the surface at once.

The candies should release if everything was done properly.

‡ Makes 24 servings.

Sea Glass Candy

Instructions

2 Cups sugar

1 Cup water

1/2 Cup corn syrup

1 Teaspoon blueberry oil flavouring

Blue food colouring

Powdered sugar

Directions

In a saucepot over medium heat, add the water, sugar and corn syrup and bring to a boil. Cook, stirring continuously until the mixture has reached 300°F.

Remove the pot from the heat and working quickly mixing in the blue food colouring and peppermint oil flavouring, stirring until fully combined. Add the amount of food colouring depending on desired color. More food colouring will lead to a darker blue candy.

Pour the sugar mixture onto a silicone lined baking sheet. Once the candy has fully cooled, break up the candy into pieces using a meat mallet.

To serve, dust half the pieces of candy with powdered sugar.

White Chocolate Blueberry Fudge

Ingredients

1/2 Stick butter

2-1/2 Cups sugar

2/3 Cup evaporated milk

1 Jar marshmallow cream

2 Small packages cream cheese

1 Package white chocolate chips

1 Cup fresh blueberries

2 Teaspoons vanilla

Directions

Place foil in the bottom and over sides of 9" square pan, leaving enough foil on sides to lift fudge when firm.

Cut cream cheese into small cubes. Rinse and drain blueberries.

Combine butter, sugar, evaporated milk, and marshmallow cream, and bring to rolling boil over medium heat. Boil for 5 minutes, stirring constantly!

Remove from heat and stir in cream cheese and white chocolate chips until melted and mixture is smooth.

Carefully stir in blueberries and vanilla.

Pour into pan and let cool. Refrigerate until firm, at least 2 hours.

Using foil "handles," lift from pan and place on cutting board.

Cut into squares and serve.

Blueberry Chocolate Clusters

Ingredients

1 Cup fresh blueberries, divided

1 Cup chocolate chips, any kind

Directions

Rinse blueberries, spread on paper towels and pat dry.

Line a baking sheet with wax paper or parchment.

In a small bowl or top of a double boiler, over barely simmering water, place chocolate. Stir until melted. Remove bowl from hot water. Gently fold in blueberries.

Make clusters by spooning 4 or 5 warm chocolate coated blueberries onto wax paper, placing them 1 inch apart or spoon mixture into silicone candy moulds.

Refrigerate until firm, about 30 minutes.

‡ Can be refrigerated in an airtight container for up to 3 days.

Chocolate Covered Blueberries

Ingredients

1 Cup semi-sweet chocolate chips

1 Tablespoon shortening

2 Cups fresh blueberries, rinsed and dried

Directions

Melt chocolate in a glass bowl in the microwave, or in a metal bowl set over a pan of simmering water. Stir frequently until melted and smooth. Remove from the heat, and stir in the shortening until melted.

Line a baking sheet with waxed paper. Add blueberries to the chocolate, and stir gently to coat. Spoon small clumps of blueberries onto the waxed paper. Refrigerate until firm, about 10 minutes. Store in a cool place in an airtight container.

‡ These will last about 2 days.

Donuts and More

Glazed Blueberry Cake Donuts

Ingredients

<u>Donut</u>

2-1/4 Cups all-purpose flour

1/3 Cup granulated sugar

1 Tablespoon baking powder

1 Teaspoon cinnamon

1/4 Teaspoon nutmeg

1/2 Teaspoon salt

4 Tablespoons unsalted butter, melted

1/2 Cup low-fat milk

1 Egg, lightly beaten

2 Teaspoons vanilla extract

1-1/2 Cups fresh blueberries

Oil for frying (about 1 quart)

<u>Glaze</u>

2 Cups powdered sugar

1-2 Tablespoons water

1 Drop of vanilla extract

Directions

<u>Donut</u>

In a large bowl, combine flour, sugar, baking powder, cinnamon, nutmeg, and salt, stirring to combine. In another bowl, combine egg, milk, and vanilla extract, mixing together. Add melted butter to the dry ingredients, quickly stirring to disperse the butter and form small crumbs. Stir in milk and egg mixture, bring the dough together with a spoon. Before it comes completely together, add in blueberries, mashing some as you go along if desired (I suggest thing!) and bring the dough together with your hands. Form it into a large ball, then roll it out on a floured surface to about 1/2-inch thickness. Cut doughnuts using a doughnut cutter, a biscuit cutter, or even a knife, using a small lid (or frosting coupler as I did) to cut out the centre. Repeat with dough scraps until all the dough is used.

Heat oil in a large pot or deep fryer, bringing it to 375°F. Fry doughnuts 1 to 2 at a time, frying for about 1-1/2 to 2 minutes per side. After your first doughnut, check it by cutting into the centre and making sure the dough is cooked through. Finish remaining doughnuts, then dip the entire thing in glaze and let sit to cool before serving.

<u>Glaze</u>

Whisk ingredients together until a smooth, runny glaze forms. If it seems too thin, add sugar a few tablespoons at a time, stirring. if it's too thick, add more water by one very small drop at a time, whisking constantly. Dunk doughnuts in the glaze and let sit to set.

Mini Blueberry Galette

Ingredients

<u>Crust</u>

1 Cup unsalted butter, cold and cut into cubes

2-1/2 Cups all-purpose flour

1 Tablespoon sugar

1 Teaspoon salt

1/2 Cup + 1 tablespoon buttermilk, cold

<u>Filling</u>

1 Pound fresh blueberries

1/3 Cup sugar

2 Tablespoons cornstarch

1/4 Teaspoon fresh ground nutmeg

Zest of 1 lemon

<u>Assembly</u>

1 Egg, for egg wash

Sanding sugar, for sprinkling

Directions

To make the pie crust, in a large bowl, stir together the flour, sugar and salt. Add the butter and toss to coat the butter. Dump entire contents of the bowl out onto a well-floured surface. With a well-floured rolling pin, roll the mixture together, flattening the butter into the flour. Use a bench scraper to bring the mixture back together again as needed. When the butter is in long sheets and evenly distributed through the flour, return the mixture to the bowl, and create a well in the centre.

Add the buttermilk to the well and use your fingers or a wooden spoon to combine. Add more buttermilk a tablespoon at a time, if necessary, but the mixture should be a little on the dry side. Dump the contents back onto your floured surface and divide into 6 disks. Wrap in plastic wrap and chill in the fridge for one hour or overnight.

To make the galettes, preheat oven to 400°F and line 2 sheet pans with parchment paper.

Combine the sugar, cornstarch, nutmeg, and lemon zest in a bowl. Add the blueberries and toss to coat. Roll out each disk of pie dough into an 8 to 10-inch circle. It doesn't need to be exact or even. Spoon 1/6 of the blueberry mixture into the centre of each disk and fold the dough up and over the filling. Brush with the dough with the egg wash and sprinkle with the sanding sugar.

Place the galettes on the prepared sheet pans and bake until crust is golden, and the filling is bubbling, about 30 to 35 minutes, rotating the sheet pans halfway through.

Serve warm or at room temperature.

‡ Can be stored in the fridge for up to 3 to 4 days.

Mini Blueberry Streusel Donuts

Ingredients

<u>Donuts</u>

1-3/4 Cup flour

2 Teaspoons baking powder

Dash of salt

1 Egg

3/4 Cup sugar

3 Tablespoons vegetable oil

1/4 Cup sour cream

1 Teaspoon vanilla

1/2 Cup whole milk

1/2 Cup frozen blueberries

<u>Streusel Topping</u>

2 Tablespoons butter, melted and cooled

1/4 Cup four

1/4 Teaspoon cinnamon

<u>Glaze</u>

2 Teaspoon whole milk

1/2 Teaspoon vanilla

3/4 Cup confectioners' sugar

Directions

Preheat the oven to 350°F. Grease a mini doughnut pan.

Whisk the flour (reserving 1 tablespoon), baking powder, and salt in a large bowl.

In another bowl combine the egg and sugar until pale yellow. Add the oil, sour cream, vanilla, and milk. Gently fold wet ingredients into the dry ingredients until everything is just moist and no lumps.

With a fork, stir together the streusel topping ingredients. Sprinkle a little into each doughnut area of the greased pan.

Toss the blueberries in the reserved 1 tablespoon of flour. Fold into the batter.

Spoon the batter into a Ziploc® bag. Snip off the edge and fill each doughnut area half full. Bake for 7 to 9 minutes. Cool on wire rack for 5 minutes before flipping pan and turning out doughnuts to cool completely on a wire rack.

Glaze

Whisk together the milk, vanilla, and confectioners' sugar. When doughnuts have cooled and are still on a wire rack, place wax paper under the rack to catch drips. Drizzle glaze over the doughnuts. Let sit for 5 minutes to set.

Fillings, Frostings, and Topping

Blueberry Perogy Filling

Ingredients

2/3 Cup sugar

1 Tablespoon all-purpose flour

2 Cups fresh or frozen (don't thaw them) blueberries

Directions

In a medium bowl, stir together the sugar and flour; stir in the blueberries. If they're frozen, store in the freezer until you're ready to use them.

‡ Makes enough for about 3 dozen perogies.

Blueberry Pie Filling

Ingredients

4 Cups blueberries (fresh or frozen)

2/3 to 1 Cup sugar

1/4 Cup lemon juice

1/4 to 1/3 Cup cornstarch (for desired filling thickness)

1/4 Cup water

Directions

In a heavy saucepan mix together blueberries, sugar and lemon juice.

Over medium heat, bring to boil, stirring frequently.

Mix cornstarch with water to make a paste.

Pour into berry mixture, stirring constantly until thick.

Remove from heat and let cool. You can now freeze it or use for pie.

Bake at 400°F for about 35 minutes.

Blueberry Ice Cream Sauce

Ingredients

1/4 Cup sugar

1 Teaspoon cornstarch

Dash salt

1/4 Cup water

1 Cup fresh or frozen blueberries

1-1/2 Teaspoons lemon juice

1/2 Teaspoon grated lemon peel

Directions

In a small saucepan, combine the sugar, cornstarch, and salt. Gradually whisk in water until smooth. Add the blueberries, lemon juice and peel; bring to a boil over medium heat, stirring constantly. Cook 2 to 3 minutes longer or until thickened, stirring occasionally (some berries will remain whole).

‡ Makes 3/4 of a cup.

Ice Creams, Sorbets, Etc.

Blueberry Mojito Popsicles

Ingredients

3-1/2 Cups fresh blueberries

1 Cup fresh mint (no stems)

3 Tablespoons agave nectar

1/2 Cup fresh lime juice

1 Lime

3 Tablespoons white rum

1-1/2 Cups carbonated water

Directions

In a blender, puree the blueberries, mint leaves, agave nectar, lime juice and zest. Add the lime and sparkling water and blend thoroughly.

Pour the mixture into popsicle moulds and add the popsicle sticks. Freeze for 4 hours or overnight.

To remove from moulds, briefly run hot water over the mould and slide the popsicles out. Wrap in plastic wrap and store in the freezer for up to 1 month.

‡ Makes 4 servings.

Blueberry Muffin Ice Cream

Ingredients

1 Batch of your favourite blueberry muffins

2 Cups whole milk

1-1/2 Tablespoons cornstarch

3 Tablespoons cream cheese softened to room temperature

1/2 Teaspoon sea salt

1/2 Teaspoon cinnamon

1-1/4 Cups heavy cream

2/3 Cups granulated sugar

2 Tablespoons light corn syrup

1 Tablespoon vanilla extract

Directions

In a small bowl, mix together 2 tablespoons of the milk with the cornstarch and whisk until smooth. Set aside. In another large bowl, whisk together softened cream cheese with salt and cinnamon until smooth.

In a large saucepan, add milk, cream, sugar, vanilla extract, and corn syrup, whisking together. Bring to a rolling boil – for me, this was over medium heat. Keep a close eye on the mixture because if it gets too hot, it will boil up and over very quickly. You want it to the point when the milk is bubbling and rolling but now boiling over. Once it comes to that point, boil for 4 minutes. I stirred occasionally here. After 4 minutes, remove from heat and very slowly whisk in the cornstarch mixture. I did it in 3 parts – adding 1/3 of it and whisking at a time. Bring back over heat and bring to a rolling boil again, this time stirring with a spatula while the mixture just thickens slightly – about 1 to 2 minutes.

Remove from heat and very slowly pour a small amount into the large bowl that has the cream cheese in it, whisking constantly until smooth. Gradually pour the rest of the mixture into the bowl while whisking to combine. Grab another very large bowl and fill it halfway full of cold water, adding a bunch of ice cubes as well. Pour the milk mixture into a 1-gallon freezer Ziploc® bag, pushing the air out and sealing it. Place it in the ice bath for 30 to 45 minutes until cold, adding more ice if needed.

Pour the ice cream mixture into your ice cream maker and churn according to the directions. After 20 to 22 minutes, add 2 to 3 crumbled blueberry muffins. Once churned to your desired consistency, place in a freezer-safe container – at this point, fold in 2 to 3 more crumbled blueberry muffins using a large spatula. Smooth out the top then place a sheet of plastic wrap over top, pressing right onto the surface. Freeze for at least 8 hours, or overnight.

Pink Grapefruit-Blueberry Sorbet

Ingredients

3 Cups fresh pink grapefruit juice

3 Cups fresh or frozen blueberries

1-1/2 Cups white sugar, or to taste

1/2 Cup vodka (optional)

Directions

Pour the grapefruit juice, blueberries, sugar, and vodka into a blender, and blend until the sugar is dissolved and the mixture is smooth 2 to 3 minutes.

Pour the mixture into a container, and freeze until solid, 3 to 4 hours. Thoroughly stir the sorbet to break up the ice crystals to a slushy consistency, and return to freezer until firm, about 3 hours. Store in the freezer in a covered container.

‡ 5 grapefruits make about 3 cups of juice.

‡ Makes 10 servings.

Roasted Blueberry Cheesecake Ice Cream

Ingredients

2 Cups fresh blueberries

1/4 Cup sugar

1 8-Ounce package of cream cheese

1 Cup whole milk

1 Cup sugar

2 Cups heavy cream

1 Teaspoon vanilla extract

Directions

Preheat oven to 375°F.

Line a rimmed cookie sheet with parchment paper.

In a bowl, combine blueberries and sugar. Toss to coat. Pour onto parchment lined cookie sheet. Place in the oven and cook for about 8 to 9 minutes.

Remove from the oven, and allow to cool completely. Place in a covered dish in the fridge until you need to mix them in the ice cream base.

Place the cream cheese in a stand mixer, whip until it's fluffy. In the same stand mixer combine the whole milk and sugar with the cream cheese, turn mixer on low and gradually increase speed to high, whisk until sugar dissolves.

Add the heavy cream and the vanilla extract. Whisk on low speed and gradually increase to high, continue whisking until mixture thickens.

Turn off mixer, and add blueberries, being careful not to splash them anywhere or your counter will be blue. Turn on the mixer, slowly, gradually increase speed.

Grab your ice cream machine bowl. It should always be in your freezer. That way it's always ready to churn. Transfer the blueberry mixture to your frozen bowl, and set that on your ice cream machine. Turn on and churn for about 10 to 15 minutes. You want it thick but still with some give. Now pop the ice cream bowl in the freezer, and cover with tinfoil or parchment with a rubber band around it. Make sure you let it set up for about 4 hours unless you want soft serve. If that's the case, use it immediately.

Marinades and Rubs

Sweet Heat Blueberry Marinade

Ingredients

1 Pint blueberries

1/3 Cup red wine vinegar

1/4 Cup peanut oil

2 Tablespoons honey

1 Teaspoon cayenne pepper

Directions

Combine all ingredients in a blender, mix well. Place selected Certified Angus Beef®
brand cut in the zipper-locking plastic bag, pour in marinade, and marinate overnight in
the refrigerator.

‡ Great with Angus beef.

‡ Makes about 2 cups.

Balsamic Blueberry Sauce

Ingredients

1 Teaspoon olive oil

2 Garlic cloves, finely minced

1/4 Vidalia onion, finely diced

6 Tablespoons balsamic vinegar

2 Tablespoons dark brown sugar

4 Teaspoons honey

2 Teaspoons molasses

2 Cups fresh blueberries

Directions

Heat olive oil in a medium saucepan over medium heat. Add garlic and onion and cook, stirring, until softened, about 5 minutes. Add remaining ingredients and stir until combined. Increase heat and bring mixture to a low boil; cook 5 minutes. Reduce heat to low, cover, and simmer 25 minutes. Keep an eye on the sauce; if it is reducing too quickly, turn the heat down or off.

Remove cover. Using the back of a wooden spoon, mash blueberries against the side of the pan to release juices. Increase heat to medium and cook until sauce reaches your preferred thickness, 6 to 8 minutes. Strain if desired and serve with steak. Makes 1-1/2 cups sauce.

‡ Works best with steak.

‡ Makes 12 servings.

Blueberry Barbecue Dry Rub

Ingredients

1 Cup Freeze-dried Blueberries, pulverized

4 Tablespoons brown sugar

1 Tablespoon kosher salt

1/2 Teaspoon black pepper

1 Tablespoon garlic powder

½ Tablespoon onion powder

1 Tablespoon dried oregano

2 Teaspoons cayenne

2 Tablespoons chilli powder

Directions

Pulverize freeze-dried blueberries in a spice grinder or mortar and pestle until blueberries resemble coarse sand. Blend together all dry-rub ingredients.

Clean and prepare your favourite BBQ cuts of meat. Thoroughly rub your cuts and allow the blueberry dry rub to penetrate for no less than 2 hours (overnight is recommended).

Prepare your BBQ or smoker. Cook your cuts over medium-low to medium heat (225°F - 250°F). When your cuts have reached the appropriate cooking temperatures, toss with additional dry-rub before serving.

Blueberry-Maple-Rosemary Sauce

Ingredients

2 Cups fresh or frozen blueberries

2 Tablespoons maple syrup

1/2 Teaspoon minced fresh rosemary

1/2 Teaspoon ground coriander

1/2 Teaspoon kosher salt

1/2 Teaspoon fresh ground black pepper

1 Tablespoon balsamic vinegar

1 Teaspoon cornstarch

Directions

Make the blueberry sauce by adding the blueberries, maple syrup, rosemary, coriander, salt, and pepper to the skillet with the pan drippings. Heat on medium-high until a few of the berries start to burst and the sauce starts to thicken a bit, about 5 minutes. Mix the balsamic vinegar with the cornstarch and add to the pan, stirring until the sauce thickens, an additional minute.

Savory Blueberry Sauce

Ingredients

2 Cups low sodium chicken broth

1/2 Medium yellow onion

1/2 Sweet apple, such as Fuji

3-4 Sprigs fresh thyme

2 Cups fresh or frozen blueberries

1-1/2 Teaspoons freshly squeezed lemon juice

1/2 Teaspoon kosher salt

1/4 Teaspoon freshly ground black pepper

3 Tablespoons unsalted butter, cut into 1/2-inch pieces

In a small saucepan, bring the chicken stock to a boil, Reduce the heat to medium and add the onion, apple, and thyme. Simmer for 30 minutes, stirring occasionally, turning over the onion and the apple until the stock is reduced by half.

With a slotted spoon, remove the onion, apple and thyme from the stock and discard. Add the blueberries and bring to a boil, Reduce the heat to medium-low and simmer for 20 minutes or until the liquid is reduced to 3/4 cup.

Remove the pan from the heat. Add the lemon juice, salt, and pepper and stir. Add the butter and whisk the sauce until the butter is completely melted, about 1 minute, Serve hot. The sauce can be made up to several days ahead, refrigerated, and gently reheated over low heat before serving.

Meats

Blueberry Barbecue Chicken

Ingredients

<u>Sauce</u>

3 Cups blueberries

2 Cups apple cider vinegar, divided

2 Cups granulated sugar

1/4 Teaspoon chilli flakes

1 3-Inch cinnamon stick

1 Bay leaf

<u>Chicken</u>

One 3-Pound chicken

3 Teaspoon kosher salt, divided

1 1/2 Teaspoon freshly ground black pepper

Directions

<u>Sauce</u>

Put the blueberries and 2 tablespoons of the vinegar in a food processor. Pulse the berries just to break them up and get some juices flowing.

In a medium saucepan, combine the pulverized berries with the remaining vinegar, sugar, chilli flakes, cinnamon stick, and bay leaf. Bring to a simmer over medium heat, reduce the heat to low, and then cover the pot. Cook for 1 hour, stirring occasionally.

Carefully transfer the hot sauce to a blender. Remove the knob from the top of the blender lid and cover with a dish towel to prevent an explosion. Blend the sauce to get it as smooth as possible, then pass it through a fine mesh strainer, directly back into the pan. Simmer the sauce over medium-low heat, stirring occasionally, until it has reduced by about 1/3 of its original volume (25 to 30 minutes). It should coat the back of a spoon and have the viscosity of maple syrup. Let the sauce rest, at least overnight, before using. This will keep for months, covered, in the refrigerator.

<u>Chicken</u>

Light your grill and heat it to roughly 350°F. Thirty minutes before you plan to grill, bring the chicken to room temperature and season with 2 teaspoons of kosher salt and the black pepper.

Place chicken, skin side up, on the grill and close the lid. Cook, covered, for 20 minutes. Baste with blueberry sauce every 5 minutes for an additional 20 minutes, keeping the lid closed between basting activity. After a total of 40 minutes, flip the chicken over to caramelize the skin, and baste the other side for 10 minutes more. Using a probe thermometer, check the internal temperature of the meaty part of a thigh. When it reaches 165°, remove chicken from the grill.

Off the grill, douse the chicken in 1/2 cup of blueberry sauce and let it rest for 10 minutes. Carve into 6 or 8 pieces and toss once more in another 1/2 cup sauce. Serve the chicken warm or at room temperature.

Blueberry-Rum Marinated Pork Tenderloin

Ingredients

1 Cup fresh blueberries

3/4 Cup rum

1/4 Cup lemon juice

2 Garlic Cloves

2 Tablespoons brown sugar

1 Tablespoon chopped sweet onion

1 Tablespoon white vinegar 1 (16-ounce)

Package pork tenderloins

French bread slices, toasted

Blueberry Salsa

Directions

Process first 7 ingredients in a blender or food processor until smooth, stopping to scrape down sides. Pour mixture into a large zip-top plastic freezer bag; add pork. Seal and chill at least 4 hours.

Remove pork from marinade, discarding marinade.

Grill pork, covered with grill lid, over medium heat (300°F to 350°F) 11 to 13 minutes on each side or until a meat thermometer inserted in thickest portion registers 155°F. Remove from grill. Loosely cover pork with foil; let stand 10 minutes or until thermometer registers 160°F. Cut pork into slices, and serve over toasted bread. Top with Blueberry salsa.

‡ For best results, marinade 24 hours before.

Bison Steak with Blueberry Marinade

Ingredients

4 Bison sirloin steaks, (or strip steaks, or rib steaks), about ½ pound each, cut about 1 inch thick

Marinade

1/3 Cup organic blueberries, fresh or frozen (thawed if frozen)

2 Tablespoons filtered water

4 Green onions, very finely chopped

3 Tablespoons unfiltered organic extra virgin olive oil

Sautéing

2 Tablespoons pastured butter

Directions

The day before you plan to cook the steaks, make the marinade. Combine the water and the blueberries in a bowl. Crush the blueberries into the water with a sturdy fork. When the blueberries are well crushed, combine with the green onions and the olive oil. Place the steaks in a glass bowl, coat all surfaces with the marinade. Cover, and let rest at room temperature for 1 hour. Refrigerate overnight.

About 1 hour before you plan to cook the steaks, remove them from the refrigerator so they can come to room temperature. When the hour is up, wipe off as much of the marinade as you can.

Heat the butter over medium heat in a heavy frying pan, preferably cast iron. When the butter is hot and slightly smoking, cook the steaks for 3 to 4 minutes on each side, until there are done to your liking.

Blueberry Grilled Chicken

Ingredients

1 Tablespoon vegetable oil

1 Tablespoon kosher salt

1 Tablespoon paprika

1 Teaspoon ground dried chipotle pepper

1/2 Teaspoon cayenne pepper

1/2 Teaspoon freshly ground black pepper

2 Cloves minced garlic

4 Skinless, boneless chicken breast halves

Blueberry Gastrique

1/3 Cup white sugar

1/3 Cup apple cider vinegar

2 Cups fresh blueberries

Salt and freshly ground black pepper to taste

Directions

Whisk oil, salt, paprika, chipotle pepper, cayenne pepper, black pepper, and garlic in a bowl to make the marinade. Place chicken breasts in marinade and turn to coat evenly. Cover the bowl with plastic wrap and refrigerate for at least 2 hours.

Spread sugar in a saucepan set over medium heat. Do not stir, but watch closely as the sugar begins to melt after about 1 minute. As the sugar melts it will gradually turn a golden colour. Continue watching but not stirring. When all sugar has melted, and golden colour just begins to darken a bit (after 1 minute or less), remove the pan from heat. Pour in vinegar and stir until sugar dissolves.

Place pan over medium-high heat and add blueberries to the sugar-vinegar mixture. Bring to a simmer, reduce heat to medium-low, and simmer until blueberries soften and mixture begins to thicken, 4 or 5 minutes. It should be a syrup-like consistency. If the sauce seems too thin, simmer a few more minutes. If it seems too thick, add a splash of water. Stir in salt and pepper. Remove from heat.

Set a strainer over a bowl. Strain berries, using a spatula to push through as much juice as possible. Discard skins.

Preheat an outdoor grill over medium-high heat and lightly oil the grate. Drain excess marinade from chicken.

Place chicken breasts on the preheated grill. Cook until no longer pink in the centre and the juices run clear, about 4 minutes per side. An instant-read thermometer inserted into the centre should read at least 165°F (74°C). Transfer chicken to a plate and allow to rest a few minutes.

Serve breasts on a swirl of blueberry sauce with more sauce drizzled on top.

Blueberry Balsamic Glazed Salmon

Ingredients

1/2 Cup fresh blueberries

5-6 Sprigs of fresh thyme

1 Tablespoon granulated sugar

1 Tablespoon balsamic vinegar

2 Teaspoon lemon juice

1/2 Teaspoon salt, divided

4 4-5 Ounces salmon filets

1/4 Teaspoon ground black pepper

Directions

In a small sauce pot, add the blueberries, thyme, sugar, balsamic vinegar, lemon juice, and 1/4 teaspoon of salt. Place over medium heat. Boil for 15 minutes, stirring occasionally. The blueberries will release their juices. The sauce will reduce and thicken.

In the meantime, place an oven rack 6 inches from the broiler. Preheat oven broiler to high. Optional: Line a baking sheet with aluminium foil.

Pat salmon filets dry with paper towels. Sprinkle both sides of the fish with a pinch of salt and pepper.

Place the fish skin side down on the baking sheet.

Brush a thin layer of the blueberry glaze onto the salmon. Place the fish under the broiler for three minutes. Brush an additional thin layer of glaze on the fish. Place back under the broiler for an additional 3 to 5 minutes. Once cooked, the salmon should flake when pressed with a fork, but not be dry.

Blueberry Coffee Rub Ingredients

Ingredients

Blueberry Coffee Rub

1/4 Cup blueberry powder, smoking optional

1/4 Cup instant espresso powder

2 Tablespoons ground coriander

2 Tablespoons ground paprika

1 Tablespoon ancho chilli powder

1 Tablespoon Kosher salt

1 Teaspoon brown sugar

1 Teaspoon dry mustard

1 Teaspoon coarse ground pepper

1/2 Teaspoon ground ginger

Rib Eye Steak

2 18-Ounce bone-in rib eye steaks

Blueberry-Coffee Rub

2 Tablespoons canola oil

3 Tablespoons butter, divided

3 Sprigs thyme, divided

1 Sprig rosemary, divided

2 Cloves garlic, smashed, divided

1/4 Cup minced shallots

1 Cup red wine

1/2 Cup beef broth

1 Cup fresh blueberries

1 Tablespoon honey

Salt and pepper, to taste

Directions

<u>Blueberry Coffee Rub</u>

In a small bowl, combine all ingredients.

<u>Blueberry Powder Smoking</u>

Place the blueberry powder onto a surgical grade screen (recommend 12x12) in a thin layer.

Preheat the smoker to get the smoke flowing. We recommend a cold smoker or a smoker that doesn't get hotter than 150°F. Chef tip: When choosing the wood type, be sure to pick a lighter wood that will allow the deep taste of the blueberry powder to shine. We suggest an Apple or Cherry wood.

Add the screen of blueberry powered to the smoker.

Cold smoke for approximately 45 minutes to 1 hour (smoke depending on desired smoke flavour)

Remove from the smoker and allow to cool to room temperature.

Once cooled, store in an airtight container in a dark, cool area.

<u>Rib Eye Steak</u>

Season both sides of steaks liberally with Blueberry Coffee Rub, store remaining dry rub in a jar for another use.

In a large heavy skillet over medium-high heat, heat canola oil. When the oil is shimmering, add steaks. Cook until browned, about 5 minutes. Turn steaks. Add 1 tablespoon of the butter, 2 sprigs of the thyme, 1/2 sprig of the rosemary and half the garlic. Cook, basting steak, until medium-rare, 3 to 5 minutes. Remove from heat; cover to keep warm.

Meanwhile, in a small skillet over medium heat, melt 1 tablespoon of the butter. Add shallots and remaining garlic. Cook, stirring frequently, until shallots are translucent, about 3 minutes. Add wine; simmer until reduced to 2 tablespoons. Add broth; simmer until reduced to 1/4 cup.

Stir in blueberries, remaining thyme and rosemary; let simmer until blueberries begin to collapse, about 5 minutes. Stir in remaining butter and the honey. Season to taste with salt and pepper. Thin sauce with a little water, if necessary.

On a cutting board, slice steak and move to a serving platter. Spoon blueberry sauce over steak.

Misc. Recipes

Blueberry Chutney

Ingredients

1 Cup blueberries

2 Green onions, chopped

1-1/2 Teaspoons grated ginger root

1/4 Cup packed brown sugar

1/4 Cup water

2 Tablespoons cider vinegar

1-1/2 Teaspoons cornstarch

Pinch salt

Directions

Combine all ingredients in a large saucepan. Bring to a boil over medium heat; stirring frequently. Cook until the mixture is the consistency of runny jam (about 3-5 minutes). Remove from heat and cool completely.

Blueberry Ketchup

Ingredients

2-1/2 Cups fresh blueberries

1 Medium shallot, minced (about 2 tablespoons)

1-1/4 Cups sugar

1/2 Cup red wine vinegar

2 Tablespoons minced fresh ginger

1 Tablespoon lime juice

1/4 Teaspoon salt

1/4 Teaspoon freshly ground pepper

Directions

Place blueberries, sugar, vinegar, ginger, lime juice, salt, and pepper in a large saucepan over medium-high heat. Stir until the sugar dissolves, about 5 minutes. Bring to a simmer, reduce heat to medium-low and simmer, stirring occasionally, until the blueberries have mostly broken down and the sauce has thickened, 20 to 30 minutes. Spoon into glass jars or a large bowl and refrigerate until chilled and thickened, about 4 hours.

‡ Makes 48 servings.

‡ Store in fridge for 2 weeks or freezer for 1 month.

Hot Blueberry Cheddar Dip with Toasty Bread

Ingredients

1 (8-Ounce) Block of cream cheese, softened

8 Ounces white cheddar cheese, freshly grated

1/4 Teaspoon nutmeg

1 Heaping cup of fresh blueberries

1 Loaf of French bread, sliced

2-3 Tablespoons olive oil

Directions

Preheat oven to 375°F. Place two oven racks in the middle and lower level. Slice bread and place on a baking sheet, drizzle it with olive oil.

In a bowl, mix cream cheese with grated cheddar and nutmeg. Fold in blueberries. Place in an oven-safe dish, then set on the top oven rack. Bake for 30 to 35 minutes, or until cheese is hot, golden, and bubbly, and blueberries and bursting. At the 20 minutes mark, place the baking sheet with bread on the lower rack to toast, checking and tossing every 4 to 5 minutes.

Spicy Chipotle Blueberry Ketchup

Ingredients

1 Pint (2 cups) fresh blueberries

1/3 Cup sugar

1/4 Cup minced onion

3 Tablespoons lime juice

3 Tablespoons white or red wine vinegar

2 to 3 Teaspoons minced chipotle pepper in adobo sauce, plus additional adobo sauce to taste

1/4 Teaspoon sea salt

1 Clove garlic, minced

Directions

Bring all ingredients to a boil in a small saucepan. Reduce heat and simmer for 30 minutes or until slightly thickened (mixture will thicken more as it cools).

Let cool, then puree in a blender or food processor.

Blueberry Mustard

Ingredients

1 Tablespoon butter

1/4 Cup finely chopped red onion

1 Clove garlic, minced

1-1/2 Cups fresh blueberries

1/4 Cup dry red wine

1 Tablespoon sugar

3 Tablespoons Dijon-style mustard

Directions

In small saucepan heat butter over medium heat. Add onion and garlic; cook and stir about 4 minutes or until onion is tender. Stir in blueberries, wine, and sugar. Bring to boiling; reduce heat. Simmer, uncovered, for 10 minutes. Mash berries lightly with a potato masher. Simmer for 2 to 4 minutes more or until thickened. Remove from heat. Stir in mustard; cool.

‡ Chill for up to 2 weeks.

Non-Alcohol Drinks

Very Berry Smoothie

Ingredients

1 Banana, chopped

1 Kiwi, sliced

3/4 Cup blueberries

1 Cup ice cubes

1 (8-Ounce) Container vanilla yoghurt

Directions

Combine the banana, kiwi, blueberries, ice cubes, and vanilla yoghurt in a blender; blend until smooth.

Blueberry-Lavender Lemonade

Ingredients

1 Cup lemon juice, fresh squeezed (about 5 to 6 lemons)

2 Cups sugar

7-1/2 Cups water, divided

1 Pint blueberries

15 Sprigs fresh lavender (1 small plant) + a few extra for garnish

Directions

In a saucepan, bring 2 cups sugar + 2 cups water to a boil.

Remove from heat, add fresh lavender sprigs and cover. Let steep for 30 minutes.

In a bowl, crush blueberries until they become a puree. You can also puree them in a blender or food processor.

You can do this next step two ways.

1. Place the blueberry-puree in a fine mesh sieve positioned over a pitcher. Remove lavender sprigs from the saucepan and pour lavender infused water through a sieve on top of the blueberry-puree and into the pitcher.
2. Remove sprigs from saucepan and place lavender infused water and blueberry-puree in a French press. Press down to create a very clear blueberry-lavender mixture.

Pour lemon juice into picture followed by 5-1/2 cups of water. Stir well! Garnish with a sprig of lavender, some floating blueberries, or a lemon slice on the glass edge.

‡ Taste lemonade in-between adding cups of water. You can also add more sugar or lemon juice at this step as well.

Avocado-Blueberry Smoothie

Ingredients

1 Cup frozen blueberries

1 (6 ounces) Container plain Greek-style yoghurt

1/2 Cup almond milk

1/2 Cup water

1/4 Avocado - peeled, pitted, and diced

Directions

Blend blueberries, yoghurt, almond milk, water, and avocado in a blender until smooth.

Almond Butter-Blueberry Smoothie

Ingredients

1 Cup almond milk

1 Cup blueberries

4 Ice cubes, or more to taste

1 Scoop vanilla protein powder

1 Tablespoon almond butter, or more to taste

1 Tablespoon chia seeds, or more to taste

Directions

Blend almond milk, blueberries, ice cubes, vanilla protein powder, almond butter, and chia seeds in a blender until smooth.

Blueberry Soda

Ingredients

20 Ounces fresh blueberries, approximately 4 cups, rinsed and drained

2 Cups water

7 Ounces sugar

1 Lime, juiced

Carbonated water

Directions

Place the blueberries and the water into a medium saucepan, set over medium-high heat and bring to a boil. Reduce the heat to low and simmer for 15 minutes. Remove the saucepan from the heat and pour the mixture into a colander lined with cheesecloth that is set in a large bowl. Allow to cool for 15 minutes. Gather up the edges of the cheesecloth and squeeze out as much of the liquid as possible. Discard the skin and pulp. Return the blueberry juice to the saucepan along with the sugar and lime juice. Place over medium-high heat and stir until the sugar has dissolved. Bring to a boil and cook for 2 minutes. Remove from the heat and transfer to a heatproof glass container and place in the refrigerator, uncovered, until completely cooled.

<u>Serve</u>

Combine 1/4 cup of the liquid with 8-ounces of carbonated water and serve over ice.

Blueberry Milk

Ingredients

1 Cup blueberries, fresh or frozen

1/4 Cup sugar

2/3 Cup water

2 Cups milk

Directions

In a small saucepan, heat blueberries, sugar and water over medium-high heat until boiling. Reduce heat to medium-low, and let simmer for 10 to 15 minutes to reduce until it thickens slightly. Remove from heat and strain through a fine-mesh strainer if desired. Refrigerate.

Whisk together 1/4 cup blueberry syrup with 1 cup cold milk to serve.

Sparkling Blueberry Lemonade

Ingredients

2/3 Cup white sugar superfine is best

2/3 Cup water

1-1/2 Cups fresh blueberries

1 Teaspoon lemon zest

1 Cup freshly squeezed lemon juice ~4 to 5 whole large lemons

2 Cups ice cubes

3 Cups sparkling water or club soda

Directions

Combine the sugar, water, blueberries, and lemon zest in a saucepan.

Bring to a boil over medium heat and then simmer for 5 to 10 minutes or until the sugar is melted and blueberries are starting to burst.

Remove from the heat and pass through a fine sieve. Let this blueberry syrup completely cool.

Meanwhile, juice the lemons to get 1 cup lemon juice.

In a large blender, add the blueberry syrup, lemon juice, and ice. Blend until smooth.

Stir in the sparkling water or club soda. Serve.

‡ Makes 6 to 8 cups.

Other Desserts

Berry Cheesecake Fluff

Ingredients

1 Box cheesecake (or vanilla) instant pudding mix (the small size)

8 Ounces cream cheese (softened)

1-1/3 Cup milk

8 Ounces Cool Whip

2 Cups chopped strawberries (patted dry)

1-1/2 Cup blueberries

Directions

In a mixing bowl, beat the dry pudding mix with the cream cheese until smooth. Slowly add milk until creamy with no lumps. Stir in cool whip and berries. Cover and chill at least 3 hours.

Blueberry Chocolate Pudding

Ingredients

Pudding

4 Tablespoons (35g/1.2oz) frozen blueberries

1/2 Teaspoon natural sweetener or other sugar

2 Tablespoons flour of choice

1/2 Tablespoon unsweetened cocoa powder

1 Tablespoon sweetener or sugar

1/2 Teaspoon instant coffee powder (optional)

1/2 Teaspoon melted coconut oil or low-fat butter

4 Tablespoons unsweetened almond milk

Sauce

1/2 Tablespoon unsweetened cocoa powder

1/2 Tablespoon brown sugar

2 Tablespoons boiling water

1 to 2 Tablespoons (extra) boiling water

Directions

Preheat oven to 390°F (200°C).

Grease a small ramekin with coconut oil spray or any cooking oil spray.

Combine the blueberries and raw sugar into the base of the ramekin.

Set aside.

In a small bowl, mix the flour, cocoa, coffee, and sweetener/sugar. Create a well in the centre, and add the melted oil/butter and milk.

Pour batter over the blueberries in the ramekin.

Make the chocolate sauce by combing cocoa powder, sugar, and water in a bowl (you can use the same bowl you used for the batter). Pour it over the cake batter and gently pour the *extra* boiling water over the back of a metal spoon over the cocoa mix.

Place ramekin into the oven and bake for approximately 15 to 20 minutes (depending on your oven) until cooked or when a toothpick inserted into the centre of the pudding comes out clean.

‡ Makes 1 serving.

Blueberry Chocolate Mousse

Ingredients

1 Punnet fresh blueberries, (7 ounces) frozen

7 Ounces dark chocolate

10 Ounces thickened cream

Directions

Scatter fresh blueberries, or some thawed frozen blueberries, over the base of 4 small-sized serving glasses and set aside.

Melt chocolate in a large heatproof bowl over a saucepan of simmering water (making sure the bowl does not touch the water). Remove and cool to room temperature.

Beat cream in a bowl to soft peaks, then fold into the melted chocolate.

Spoon the mousse among serving glasses over the blueberries and serve immediately.

‡ Makes 4 servings.

Chocolate Blueberry Pie

Ingredients

6 Cups wild blueberries

1/2 Cup sugar

3-1/2 Ounces chopped dark chocolate

Juice of half a lemon

2 Pre-made pie dough crusts

Butter for brushing

Directions

Preheat oven to 350°F.

Line a 9-inch pie plate with one of the crusts.

In a large bowl, mash blueberries with a fork to get the juices flowing. You don't want them too mashed, leave most of them whole.

Pour sugar and lemon juice over blueberries and let sit about 10 minutes. If the mixture is too watery remove some of the liquid. I removed about 1/2 a cup. Mix in the chocolate and pour the mixture into the prepared pie pan.

Top with remaining crusts and pinch the rim of the crusts together. Brush with a light coat of butter.

Bake for 60 to 65 minutes or until golden (if the edges start to get too dark wrap aluminium foil around them).

Let sit for about 15 minutes before serving.

Blueberry Pie

Ingredients

3/4 Cup white sugar

3 Tablespoons cornstarch

1/4 Teaspoon salt

1/2 Teaspoon ground cinnamon

4 Cups fresh blueberries

9-Inch double crust pie

1 Tablespoon butter

Directions

Preheat oven to 425°F (220°C).

Mix sugar, cornstarch, salt, and cinnamon, and sprinkle over blueberries.

Line pie dish with one pie crust. Pour berry mixture into the crust, and dot with butter. Cut remaining pastry into 1/2 to 3/4-inch wide strips and make a lattice top. Crimp and flute edges.

Bake pie on lower shelf of the oven for about 50 minutes, or until crust is golden brown.

Pie Crust

Ingredients

2-1/2 Cups all-purpose flour, plus extra for rolling

1 Cup (2 sticks or 8 ounces) unsalted butter, very-cold, cut into 1/2-inch cubes

1 Teaspoon salt

1 Teaspoon sugar

6 to 8 Tablespoons ice water

Directions

Put flour, sugar, and salt into the bowl of a food processor and pulse a couple times to mix. Add about half of the butter to the food processor and pulse several times. Then add the rest of the butter and pulse 6 to 8 times until the largest pieces of butter are about the size of large peas. Sprinkle the mixture with about 1/4 cup of ice water (make sure there are no ice cubes in the water!) and pulse again. Then add more ice water, a tablespoon at a time, pulsing once or twice after each addition until the dough just barely begins to hold together.

The mixture is ready if when you pinch some of the crumbly dough together with your fingers, it holds together. Watch the amount of water you add because too much and the crust will be tough.

Carefully empty the crumbly dough mixture from the food processor on to a clean, dry, flat surface. Gather the mixture in a mound. Push down with the palm of your hand on the dough crumbles a few times. This will help flatten the pieces of butter into layers which will help your crust be flaky.

Divide the dough mixture into two even-sized mounds. Use your hands to form each one into a disk. Do not over-knead! Kneading develops gluten which will toughen the dough, not something you want in a pastry crust.

If you started with cold butter you should be able to see small chunks of butter speckling the dough. This is a good thing. These small bits of butter will spread out into layers as the crust cooks, so you have a flaky crust!

Sprinkle each disk with a little flour, wrap each one in plastic wrap, and refrigerate for one hour or up to 2 days.

Remove one crust disk from the refrigerator. Let sit at room temperature for 5 to 10 minutes to soften just enough to make rolling out a bit easier. Roll out with a rolling pin on a lightly floured surface to a 12-inch circle; about 1/8 of an inch thick. As you roll out the dough, check if the dough is sticking to the surface below. If necessary, add a few sprinkles of flour under the dough to keep the dough from sticking. Carefully place onto a 9-inch pie plate. Gently press the pie dough down so that it lines the bottom and sides of the pie plate. Use a pair of kitchen scissors to trim the dough to within 1/2 inch of the edge of the pie dish.

Add filling to the pie.

Roll out the second disk of dough, as before. Gently place onto the top of the filling in the pie. Pinch top and bottom of dough rounds firmly together. Trim excess dough with kitchen shears, leaving a 3/4-inch overhang. Fold the edge of the top piece of dough over and under the edge of the bottom piece of dough, pressing together. Flute edges using thumb and forefinger or press with a fork. Score the top of the pie with four 2-inch long cuts, so that steam from the cooking pie can escape.

Salads

Blueberry Feta Salad with Lemon-Poppy Seed Dressing

Ingredients

6 Cups mixed greens

1 Cup blueberries

4 Ounce crumbled feta cheese

1/4 Cup almonds

Red onion slivers to taste

Dressing

1/3 Cup olive oil

1/3 Cup golden balsamic vinegar

1 Tablespoon lemon juice

1 Tablespoon honey

1 Teaspoon poppy seeds

1/4 Teaspoon pepper

Directions

Layer salad ingredients in large salad bowl or platter.

Prepare the dressing by combining all ingredients in a container with a lid; shake vigorously to combine.

Toss salad with dressing.

Blueberry Arugula Salad with Honey-Lemon Dressing

Ingredients

<u>Dressing</u>

1-1/2 Tablespoons lemon juice from 1/2 of a medium-size lemon

1 Small clove garlic minced

1/8 Teaspoon sea salt

2 Tablespoons honey

1/4 Cup extra virgin olive oil

Freshly ground black pepper

<u>Almonds</u>

1/2 Cup sliced almonds

1 Tablespoon honey

1 Teaspoon melted butter

1/2 Teaspoon extra virgin olive oil

1/8 Teaspoon sea salt

<u>Salad</u>

5 Ounces baby arugula

1-1/2 Cups fresh blueberries

2 to 3 Ounces goat cheese (optional)

1/2 Cup sweet almonds

Directions

For the almonds, preheat oven to 350°F.

Place honey, butter, olive oil and almonds in a medium-size oven-safe pan. Stir to combine and spread to an even layer.

Bake for 8 minutes or until light golden brown, stirring after the first five minutes.

Turn almonds out onto a sheet of parchment paper and spread out with a spatula. Cool completely, then store in an airtight container.

For the dressing, combine lemon juice garlic and salt in a small bowl. Let sit for about 5 minutes. The lemon juice will soften and mellow the garlic, so be sure to let it sit for this short period.

Add the honey and stir well. Add the olive oil in a slow drizzle, stirring continuously with a small whisk or fork. Taste and if it's too tart add a bit more honey and olive oil. If it's too bland, add a bit more lemon juice. Add freshly ground black pepper, to taste.

For the salad, place arugula in a salad bowl. Add 2 tablespoons of the dressing and toss to coat the leaves.

Scatter the blueberries, goat cheese and almonds over the top. Serve immediately.

Blueberry Quinoa Salad

Ingredients

Salad

1/2 Cup dry quinoa (red or white)

1 Cup vegetable stock (or sub water, but it will have less flavour)

5 Ounces mixed salad greens

1/2 Cup roasted unsalted hazelnuts

1/2 Cup blueberries

Dressing

1 Tablespoon grapeseed oil

2 Shallots, minced (or 1/2 cup sweet yellow onion)

1/3 Cup balsamic vinegar

1 Tablespoon maple syrup (or honey)

1 to 2 Tablespoons olive oil (or more grapeseed oil)

Pinch each salt and pepper

1/3 Cup blueberries

Directions

Prepare quinoa by rinsing thoroughly with cool water through a fine mesh strainer. Then add to a small saucepan with vegetable stock (or water) and bring to a boil over high heat.

Once boiling, reduce heat to low, cover, and simmer for 15 to 20 minutes, or until liquid is absorbed and quinoa is fluffy like rice. Remove from heat and set aside to cool slightly.

In the meantime, prepare dressing by heating a small skillet over medium heat. Once hot, add 1 tablespoon grapeseed oil, shallot, and sauté until tender and slightly caramelized - about 5 minutes - stirring often. Remove from heat to cool.

Add shallot to a food processor or blender with balsamic vinegar, olive oil, blueberries, maple syrup, and a pinch each salt and pepper. Blend until pureed, scraping down sides as needed. Taste and adjust seasonings as needed.

To plate, top the mixed greens with slightly cooled quinoa (you may not use it all), blueberries and hazelnuts. Serve with dressing.

‡ Serves 2 as an entrée, 4 as a side dish.

Blueberry Walnut Salad

Ingredients

1 (10 ounces) Package mixed salad greens

1 Pint fresh blueberries

1/4 Cup walnuts

1/2 Cup raspberry vinaigrette salad dressing

1/4 Cup crumbled feta cheese

Directions

In a large bowl, toss the salad greens with the blueberries, walnuts, and raspberry vinaigrette. Top with feta cheese to serve.

Blueberry Gelatin Salad

Ingredients

1 Can (8 ounces) crushed pineapple in juice

2 Packages (6 ounces) blackberry gelatin (or black cherry or black raspberry)

3 Cups water, boiling

1 Can (5 ounces) blueberries, drained

1 Cup sour cream

1 Package (8 ounces) cream cheese, softened

1/2 Cup sugar

<u>Garnish</u>

Chopped walnuts or pecans

Directions

Drain pineapple; reserve juice.

Dissolve the gelatin in boiling water; stir in reserved pineapple juice. Chill until slightly set, about the consistency of unbeaten egg white.

Stir in pineapple and blueberries. Pour into a 9-1/2x6x2-inch pan; chill until firm.

In a bowl, combine sour cream, cream cheese, and sugar; mix well until smooth and well blended. Spread over blueberry salad and then top with chopped pecans or walnuts.

‡ Chill thoroughly before garnishing.

Blueberry-Pineapple Salad

Ingredients

4 Cups fresh blueberries

1 Cup fresh pineapple, chopped

1/4 Cup very finely diced celery

4 Ounces cream cheese

1/2 Cup plain Greek yoghurt

1/4 Cup toasted walnuts, chopped (can also use slivered almonds)

1 Teaspoon fresh lemon zest

1 Teaspoon lemon juice

1 Teaspoon vanilla extract

2 to 3 Tablespoons honey

1 Teaspoon fresh lemon thyme and more for garnish (optional)

Directions

Blend yoghurt, cream cheese, honey, lemon zest, lemon juice, honey, lemon thyme (if using) and vanilla in the bowl of an electric mixer until smooth and creamy

Stir in remaining ingredients and garnish with a sprig of lemon thyme, if desired.

Cover and chill until ready to serve.

Sauces, Syrups, and Dressings

Blueberry Balsamic Vinaigrette Salad Dressing

Ingredients

1/4 Cup blueberries

1/4 Cup balsamic vinegar

1/2 Tablespoon honey or maple syrup

1/2 Tablespoon Dijon mustard

1/4 Cup olive oil

Salt and pepper

Directions

Combine the ingredients in a blender or food processor and puree until smooth. Season to taste with salt and pepper. Store in the refrigerator.

Blueberry Sauce

Ingredients

3 Cups blueberries (fresh or frozen)

1 Cup water

1/2 Cup sugar

1-1/2 Tablespoons cornstarch dissolved into 3 tablespoons water

1/2 Teaspoon vanilla

Directions

Place 1-1/2 cups blueberries in a small saucepan. Cover with water and add sugar and vanilla. Heat over medium-high heat until mixture comes to a low boil and blueberries just start to break apart.

Add dissolved cornstarch to the saucepan and bring mixture to a rolling boil. Turn heat down and simmer on low heat for 2 to 3 minutes, or until sauce reaches desired consistency. Add water, one tablespoon at a time, if the sauce gets too thick.

Remove from heat. Add remaining blueberries and stir gently. Serve warm or cold.

Blueberry Syrup

Ingredients

2 Cups blueberries, fresh or frozen

1/2 Cup sugar or honey

1 Cup + 2 tablespoons water, divided

1 Tablespoon cornstarch (or tapioca starch for grain-free)

Directions

Combine 2 Tablespoons water and cornstarch in a small dish and set aside.

In a medium saucepan, bring water, sugar or honey, and blueberries to a boil. Stir occasionally. Reduce heat and simmer for about 10 minutes. Add water and starch mixture and blend well. The sauce will thicken, the blueberries will have busted open and it begins to smell like pie.

Store in refrigerator up to two weeks. Take out a few minutes before serving at room temperature or warm.

Blueberry Vinaigrette

Ingredients

1/2 Cup blueberries (fresh or frozen)

1/4 Cup white vinegar

1/4 Cup honey

6 Tablespoons extra virgin olive oil

Directions

In a blender or food processor, combine all ingredients.

Blend until well combined and smooth.

Refrigerate until ready to serve.

‡ Makes 4 to 6 servings.

Blueberry Drink Syrup for Ice Tea

Ingredients

4 Cups fresh blueberries or 4 cups dry-packed frozen blueberries, rinsed and drained

2 Cups water

1 Cup sugar

Directions

Place blueberries in a saucepan with water. Bring to a boil, reduce heat and simmer 10 minutes.

Set sieve or colander lined with cheesecloth (I use a thick paper towel) over a bowl and pour in the blueberry mixture.

Gently press out the juice with a spoon or by twisting the cheesecloth. Discard the pulp and measure the juice into a saucepan.

Add 1/2 cup sugar for each cup of juice and cook over medium heat, stirring until sugar is dissolved.

Bring to a boil and cook 2 minutes.

Chill and pour into a covered jar. Store in refrigerator.

Add two tablespoons to each glass of prepared iced tea. Stir well and garnish with a lemon slice.

Maple Blueberry Balsamic Salad Dressing

Ingredients

1/2 Cup fresh or frozen blueberries

1/4 Cup olive oil

2 Tablespoon balsamic vinegar

1 to 2 Cloves garlic

2 Tablespoon maple syrup

Salt & pepper, pinch of each

Directions

Put all ingredients into a blender and blend until creamy. Serve with your favourite salad

‡ Makes about 10 servings.

Blueberry Simple Syrup

Ingredients

1 Cup blueberries

1 Cup warm water

1 Cup white sugar

1 Teaspoon lemon juice

Directions

Mix blueberries, water, and sugar together using a whisk in a small saucepan over low heat until sugar is dissolved, about 5 minutes. Increase heat to medium and bring a gentle boil, stirring often, until syrup is thickened about 15 minutes.

Whisk lemon juice into syrup; serve immediately or cool.

Blueberry Chili Hot Sauce

Ingredients

1 Cup hot chilli peppers, stem and seeds removed and coarsely chopped

2 Cups fresh or frozen blueberries, coarsely chopped

3 Cloves garlic, chopped

1/4 Cup onions, diced

1 Plum tomato, skin removed and diced

8 Whole cloves

3/4 Cup distilled white vinegar

1/2 Teaspoon kosher salt.

4 Teaspoons sugar

Directions

Once the mixture begins to bubble, reduce heat to low, cover and continue to simmer until peppers are tender—about 10 minutes.

Take the sauce off the heat and let it cool until it's at a safe temperature for handling. Pour into a blender and purée.

Pour the sauce into a 2-cup size glass or ceramic bowl and let it sit (with a loose paper towel on top) until cool.

The sauce may be used as a thick puree OR strain through a fine sieve or food mill if you prefer it more of a liquid hot sauce.

‡ Keep refrigerated in a sealed jar. Will last up to three months.

‡ Makes about 1-1/2 cups.

‡ The heat depends on the heat of the chillies you use. You can always replace some of the chillies with sweet red peppers if you'd like to tone down the heat.

Soups

Blueberry Soup

Ingredients

3 Cups blueberries, fresh or frozen

2 Tablespoons honey

2 Teaspoons lemon juice

1 Cinnamon stick

2 Teaspoons Cornstarch

1 Teaspoon lemon zest

Yogurt for serving, if desired

Mint leaf for garnish, optional

Directions

Combine the berries with the honey, lemon juice, cinnamon stick, and a cup of water. Bring to a gentle boil, then turn down to a low simmer, cover and cook 8 to 10 minutes, until the berries are stewed. Strain the berry skins out and just use the juice or leave them in for more texture.

Stir the cornstarch into 1 tablespoon of warm water to make a slurry, then stir this into the cooked berries. Bring back to a very gentle boil and cook, stirring, until starting to thicken, about 2 minutes. Remove from the heat and stir in the lemon zest.

Serve warm, or chill and serve later. Top with a scoop of yoghurt before serving (or use whipped cream or creme fraiche instead of yoghurt if you'd like to make this a dessert).

Scandinavian Blueberry Soup

Ingredients

1 (1 Pound) Bag unsweetened frozen blueberries

1 Cup water

5 Tablespoons sugar

2 Lemon slices (1/4-inch thick)

1 Cinnamon stick

1 Pinch salt

1/2 Teaspoon vanilla extract

Lemon wedge

Low-fat vanilla yoghurt or vanilla frozen yoghurt

Directions

Bring first 7 ingredients to boil in a heavy medium saucepan over high heat, stirring until sugar dissolves. Reduce heat to medium-low and simmer until berries are very tender about 15 minutes. Discard lemon slices and cinnamon stick.

Puree half of soup in blender or processor. Transfer all the soup to medium bowl and refrigerate until very cold. (Can be prepared 2 days ahead.).

Divide soup between 2 bowls or large goblets. Serve with lemon wedges and a dollop of vanilla yoghurt.

‡ Makes 2 to 3 servings.

Blueberry-Thyme Soup with Honey Vanilla Mascarpone

Ingredients

Blueberry–Thyme Soup

6 Cups (about 3 pints) fresh blueberries

2 Cups water

3/4 Cup sugar

1 Lemon, zested

1 Tablespoon fresh thyme, finely chopped

Pinch of Kosher Salt

Honey-Vanilla Mascarpone

8 Ounces mascarpone cheese

1 Tablespoon honey

1 Teaspoon vanilla extract

1/2 – 1 Lemon, juiced

Garnish

Fresh blueberries

Crushed graham crackers or crushed shortbread cookies, optional

Directions

In a medium pot, add the blueberries (keep a few of the blueberries to the side for garnish), water, sugar, zest of one lemon, fresh thyme, and a dash of salt. Stir to combine.

Bring the pot to a boil over medium heat then lower to a gentle simmer, stirring occasionally. Cook until the blueberries start to break down and the mixture thickens slightly approximately 20 to 30 minutes.

Allow blueberry mixture to cool, then transfer to a blender (or use one of those fancy immersion blenders I love so much). Puree until smooth (make sure if the mixture is still warm while blending, hold the top of the blender down to prevent the steam from popping the lid off).

Place a fine-mesh sieve over a bowl. Transfer the blueberry mixture from the blender into the sieve (in batches if your sieve doesn't hold the full amount). Use a spoon or spatula and stir the mixture through the sieve, discarding the solids. Chill the soup until ready to serve (up to a day ahead of time).

Before serving, make the Honey Vanilla Mascarpone. Combine the mascarpone cheese, honey, vanilla extract, and the juice of 1/2 lemon. Stir to combine and taste. If you taste a hint of lemon, you're good. If you prefer a little more lemon taste, add the juice from the other 1/2 of lemon.

To plate, add the blueberry soup, a dollop (or quenelle, if you want to be fancy) of the honey-vanilla mascarpone, a couple fresh blueberries, and a sprinkle of the crushed graham crackers/shortbread cookies (optional).

Banana-Blueberry Soup

Ingredients

2 Bananas

1 Cup blueberries

6-3/4 Ounces buttermilk

Directions

Slice the banana and freeze for a couple of hours.

Put the banana, blueberries and buttermilk in a blender and blend to make a thick liquid.

Serve in bowls with a few extra blueberries to garnish. If you're not serving it immediately, keep it chilled in the fridge.

‡ Makes 2 to 4 servings.

Blueberry-Beet Soup Recipe

Ingredients

2 Tablespoons peanut oil

1 Medium onion, finely diced

1 Celery rib, finely diced

2 Tablespoons butter

2 Tablespoons honey

4 to 5 Cups chicken broth

3/4 Cup plus 1/4 cup blueberries

1 Cup cooked beets, chopped

1/4 to 1/2 Cup crème fraiche or thick plain yoghurt

Directions

In a medium saucepan with Teflon™ non-stick coatings, heat the oil over medium and sauté onion and celery 2 minutes; melt in butter and honey. Heat through and add the broth, 3/4 cup of the blueberries and the beets. Cook 20 minutes to absorb flavours. Transfer to a blender and process to smooth. Transfer to serving bowls and garnish each with a few berries. Using a piping bag, shape the crème fraiche into a heart, if desired. Serve room temperature.

Mustikkakeitto (Finnish Blueberry Soup)

Ingredients

3 Pints blueberries (about 4 cups)

¾ Cup sugar

1 Stick cinnamon

Zest and juice of 1 lemon

2 Tablespoon cornstarch

Kosher salt, to taste

Whipped cream, for serving

Directions

Bring blueberries and 3 cups water to a boil in a 4-quart saucepan over high heat; reduce heat to medium and cook, stirring occasionally until berries begin to burst, about 12 minutes. Strain, saving cooking liquid, and using a spoon, gently press the berries to extract all their juice; discard berries. Return liquid to saucepan; add sugar, cinnamon, zest, and juice; bring to a boil. Mix cornstarch and 2 tablespoons water in a bowl; add to pan and cook, while stirring, until soup is thick, 3 to 5 minutes. Discard cinnamon; season with salt and serve with whipped cream.

‡ Makes 4 to 6 servings.

Blueberry-Apple Soup

Ingredients

2 Cups fresh blueberries

Juice of 1-1/2 limes

1/2 Teaspoon cinnamon

1 Teaspoon coriander

2 Teaspoon agave nectar

1/4 Cup frozen unsweetened apple juice concentrate

1/4 Cup non-fat plain Greek yoghurt

Pinch of kosher salt

Mint leaves, for garnish (optional)

Directions

In the work bowl of a food processor fitted with a metal blade, purée the blueberries with the lime juice. Pour the mixture through a strainer, pressing gently with a wooden spoon, to extract the purée without most of the seeds. Wipe the food processor bowl with a paper towel, and return the purée to the processor.

Add the cinnamon, coriander, agave, frozen apple juice concentrate and yoghurt, and process until smooth. Stir in a pinch of kosher salt.

Chill the soup for at least 1 hour before serving, or store in a container with a tight-fitting lid for up to 2 days. Garnish individual portions with fresh mint leaves.

‡ Makes 4 servings.

‡ Can be used as an appetizer or dessert.

Spiced Blueberry Soup

Ingredients

2 Cardamom pods, (optional)

2 Tablespoons cornstarch

1/3 Cup low-fat milk

1 Cup 4 teaspoons reduced-fat sour cream, divided

Directions

Combine blueberries, water, cinnamon stick, honey, ginger, and cardamom pods (if using) in a large saucepan. Bring to a boil, stirring occasionally. Reduce heat and simmer, stirring, until most of the blueberries have burst, 1 to 2 minutes. Remove the cardamom pods and cinnamon stick. Puree the soup in 2 batches in a blender until smooth (use caution when pureeing hot liquids). Place a fine sieve over the pan and pour the soup through it back into the pan, straining out any solids. (Discard the solids.) Whisk cornstarch and milk in a measuring cup until smooth. Whisk into the blueberry mixture. Bring the soup to a boil over medium heat, stirring. Boil, stirring constantly, until the soup thickens slightly, about 1 minute. Remove from the heat and let cool for 10 minutes. Transfer to a bowl, loosely cover and chill until cold, at least 5 hours or up to 2 days. Just before serving, whisk 1 cup sour cream into the soup and ladle into bowls; top each serving with 1/2 teaspoon sour cream and swirl decoratively into the soup. Garnish with additional blueberries, if desired.

‡ Can be refrigerated for up to 5 days.

‡ Makes 1/2 cup serving.

Blueberry Gazpacho Recipe

Ingredients

4 Pints fresh blueberries

2 Yellow peppers – small dice

3 Red peppers – small dice

1 Cup creme fraiche

1/2 Cup champagne vinegar

2-1/2 Cups 1" cubed bread (any kind)

Butter (for sautéing bread cubes)

Thyme (for seasoning bread cubes)

1-1/2 Cups water

1/2 Cup heavy cream

1/4 Cup sugar

1/4 Cup olive oil

Tad of aged sherry vinegar for a drizzle finish before serving

Directions

Combine all other ingredients (except aged sherry vinegar) into a large bowl. Marinade at room temperature for 1 to 6 hours.

In a skillet, toast bread cubes with some butter & thyme. Make croutons. Set aside.

When marinade is complete, blend mixture in a blender – in small batches.

Serve chilled with a topping of croutons and drizzle of aged sherry vinegar.

Butternut Squash Soup with Blueberry Relish

Ingredients

4 Cups butternut squash

1 Teaspoon cinnamon

1 Tablespoon extra virgin olive oil

2 Apple, peeled, cored, and sliced

1 Sweet onion, diced

1 Tablespoon grated ginger

4 Cups organic vegetable broth

1 Teaspoon sea salt

1/8 Teaspoon cayenne pepper

Relish

1 Cup frozen blueberries

1/2 Apple, peeled, cored, and finely diced

1/2 Navel orange, finely diced

1 Tablespoon orange zest

Pinch sea salt

1 Teaspoon sugar

Directions

Preheat oven to 425°F. Cut squash in half lengthwise and scoop out the seeds.

Place on a baking sheet with the flesh side up. Sprinkle with cinnamon and bake in the oven for 45 minutes or until tender. Remove squash from oven and let cool. Use a spoon to carve out the flesh and set aside. Discard the skin.

Heat olive oil in a large pot over medium heat. Add the apples, onion and ginger and sauté for about 5 minutes or until soft. Add the vegetable broth, cooked squash, sea salt and cayenne pepper. Reduce heat to a simmer for about 10 minutes.

In a small bowl, combine all the ingredients for the Wild Blueberry relish and mix well. Transfer soup to a blender or use an immersion blender to puree until the soup reaches a smooth, thick consistency. Keep blending until the soup thickens, it may take some time.

Divide soup between serving bowls. Add 2 tablespoons of Wild Blueberry relish to the centre of each soup bowl. Serve immediately while soup is hot.

Honeydew-Blueberry Soup

Ingredients

1 Honeydew melon

1 Pint blueberries

6 Oatmeal cookies

Directions

Cut the melon from the rind and into chunks. Puree until smooth in a food processor or blender. Pour into a large bowl and stir blueberries into the pureed melon. Chill until quite cold.

To serve, ladle soup into individual bowls and crumble an oatmeal cookie over each serving.

‡ Makes 6 servings.

Scandinavian Blueberry Bisque

Ingredients

4 Cups fresh or frozen blueberries

6 Cups orange juice

1/4 Cup firmly-packed light brown sugar

1/4 Teaspoon ground cinnamon2 tablespoons cornstarch

2 Tablespoons water

3/4 Teaspoon grated orange peel

Sour cream or Greek yoghurt, for garnish

Directions

In a large saucepan, combine blueberries, orange juice, brown sugar, and cinnamon. Bring to a boil.

In a small bowl, combine cornstarch and water; gradually stir into blueberry mixture.

Cook, stirring frequently until mixture comes to a simmer and thickens slightly.

Remove from heat; stir in orange peel.

Let cool 15 minutes.

In a blender, puree in batches in a blender; pour into a bowl. Cover and chill.

Serve soup cold with a swirl of sour cream and a few blueberries, if desired.

‡ Makes 8 servings.

Blueberry-Lavender Soup

Ingredients

16 Cups fresh blueberries

1 Cup red wine

3 Cups water

1-1/2 Cup sugar

1/2 Cup orange juice concentrate

2-1/2 Tablespoons dried lavender

3 Lemons juice and rind

2 Cinnamon sticks

1 Teaspoon ground cloves

1 Teaspoon salt & pepper

Directions

Place all ingredients in a stockpot. Bring just to a boil, reduce heat and simmer 10 minutes.

Garnish with fresh blueberries and lavender flowers. Serve hot or cold.

Blueberry-Buttermilk Soup

Ingredients

2 Cups blueberries, washed

1-1/2 Cups water

1/2 Cup sugar

1/2 Teaspoon orange zest, grated

2 Tablespoons orange juice

2 Cups buttermilk

1 Orange, sliced

Directions

Set aside a few blueberries for garnish.

Combine remaining berries, water, sugar, orange rind and orange juice in a saucepan. Bring to a boil. Cover and reduce heat. Simmer 20 minutes.

Cool. Press blueberries through a sieve or purée until smooth in a blender. Stir in buttermilk.

Chill until icy cold. Over each serving float, orange slice topped with a few blueberries.

‡ Makes 5 servings.

www.ingramcontent.com/pod-product-compliance
Lightning Source LLC
Chambersburg PA
CBHW081149090426
42736CB00017B/3243